A World for My Daughter

Caitlin Press Inc.
8100 Alderwood Road,
Halfmoon Bay, BC V0N 1Y1
www.caitlin-press.com

Text and cover design by Vici Johnstone
Cover image Alejandro Frid
Printed in Canada

Caitlin Press Inc. acknowledges financial support from the Govern-
ment of Canada and the Canada Council for the Arts, and from the
Province of British Columbia through the British Columbia Arts
Council and the Book Publisher's Tax Credit.
Library and Archives Canada Cataloguing in Publication

Canada Council   Conseil des Arts   BRITISH COLUMBIA   Canadä Canadä
for the Arts   du Canada   ARTS COUNCIL

Frid, Alejandro, 1964-, author
    A world for my daughter : an ecologist's search for optimism
/ Alejandro Frid.

ISBN 978-1-927575-96-3 (paperback)

    1. Frid, Alejandro, 1964-. 2. Ecologists—Canada—Biography.
3. Fathers and daughters—Canada—Biography. 4. Human ecology.
5. Optimism. I. Title.

QH31.F75A3 2015   577.092   C2015-903564-3

A World for My Daughter

AN ECOLOGIST'S SEARCH FOR OPTIMISM

Alejandro Frid

CAITLIN PRESS

For Gail and Twyla Bella.

Contents

15—INTRODUCTION

Breaking the Surface

19—PROLOGUE

A Letter to the Future

25—CHAPTER 1

Storms and Stillness

41—CHAPTER 2

Vanishing Glimpses

57—CHAPTER 3

Vibrant Tension

77—CHAPTER 4

Climate and War

93—INTERLUDE

The Genius Who Invented Walking

129—CHAPTER 5

Wild Food

153—CHAPTER 6

Ever Try to De-acidify an Ocean?

183—CHAPTER 7

Irrevocable Change

193—EPILOGUE

A Birth Story

197—AFTERWORD

199—ACKNOWLEDGEMENTS

201—NOTES

212—SELECTED BIBLIOGRAPHY

220—PHOTO INFORMATION

224—ABOUT THE AUTHOR

Breaking the Surface

October 27, 2009. A clear and cool autumn day in Howe Sound, a deep-water fjord right on the edge of Vancouver, in the company of marine biologists Jeff Marliave and Donna Gibbs. I was working with the Vancouver Aquarium Marine Science Centre and—lucky us—it was another day at the job.

You see, Jeff had become fascinated with bioherms: reefs of glass sponges living on layers of dead sponges. This is ancient stuff, dating back to the Jurassic period, more than 145 million years ago. Most bioherms are very deep, inaccessible to divers. But—much to our excitement—some unusually shallow ones had been discovered recently in Howe Sound. The plan was for Donna and me to dive a bioherm off southeast Gambier Island and document its fish and invertebrate life.

I had been working with Donna and Jeff for a year and a half, making hundreds of dives to study lingcod and rockfish. For the most part, my analyses were showing an absence of large fish, reflecting a history of overfishing. I had also immersed myself in the scientific literature on climate change and ocean acidification, two major stressors which, combined with overfishing, are altering the world's seas irrevocably.

Back then my daughter, Twyla Bella, was five and a half. Watching her grow up, I could not stop thinking about how the ocean supports most life on Earth, including us, yet is suffering severe collateral damage from our carbon-intensive economy.

That is the kind of understanding that, if you are not careful, gives you licence to give up. Had you burrowed yourself into my psyche that day, you would have seen a sort of ping-pong match between my nihilistic demons and that struggling part of me that wanted to gift Twyla Bella with genuine optimism.

We approached the site. Jeff piloted the dive skiff and, after slowing down and turning on the GPS and depth sounder, launched into classic Jeff Marliave theatrics. That is, he hollered, at the top of his lungs, our depth relative to the target: "60 metres, 80 metres, 50 metres…too deep!" And so forth, with plenty of colourful language interjected here and there, until he nailed the spot and yelled at me to drop overboard the weighted line which, once suspended from a surface float, would guide our long descent through the water column.

Shortly afterwards, the float stood straight up, immobile. No current at all. Unusual in this often-tumultuous part of the sound, yet exactly what we needed for this dive.

After donning scuba gear, Donna and I rolled backwards into the water. While still at the surface, I looked down towards the bottom and almost lost my regulator as my jaw dropped open. Thirty-three metres below—past the far reach of streaming sun rays—I could see the white expanse of the bioherm.

Staring through that extraordinarily clear water, I felt as if I was inside an ethereal womb, filled with certainty that, no matter the damage wrought by overfishing and climate change, the moment was as real as it gets.

So we plummeted. Straight towards the bottom, until we broke our freefall with short blasts of air into our dry suits, mere centimetres above the convoluted, maze-like towers of glass sponges.

In the quiet buzz of controlled adrenalin, we set to work. Donna documenting tiny shrimps, some with melodic names like *Eualus*, *Heptacarpus*, *Lebbeus*. Me, I just counted fish.

Everywhere around me were quillback rockfish, my spiny friends whose intense blacks and yellows beckoned me to go deeper and closer; I love the fact that they can live almost a century, if given a break from fishing. Puget Sound rockfish, orange-red, tiny, hiding in sponge cavities. Lingcod, the largest predatory fish on these reefs. Throughout the dive, a harbour seal swam about twenty metres to the side of us, perhaps feeding. And it went on and on.

Inevitably, as nitrogen built in our blood and the air pressure in our tanks dropped, we began to rise. The trip up was slow and, with no current to sweep us sideways, we could control our movements without having to hang on to the guide line or kick our fins. We floated up in peaceful space, lifted passively by the air inside our dry suits which we released, in small bursts through a valve, as it expanded under the lower water pressure of shallower depths. The bubbles that we exhaled were the only sound, yet the speechless conversation was very animated. Staring down, we regained a panoramic view of the white expanse of glass sponges and the dark shapes of hovering rockfish.

Ten metres from the surface we entered a thick aggregation of *Nanomia bijuga*: tailed jellies the length of my forearm and shaped like snakes, their star-like organs held inside translucent bodies. A living constellation.

All of this a mere twenty-three kilometres from downtown in Western Canada's largest city. All of this amidst acidifying oceans and rising concentrations of atmospheric carbon dioxide.

Bioherm. Rockfish. *Nanomia*. Who would have believed that they were still here?

Bioherm. Rockfish. *Nanomia*. What do they have to say about the world that will be handed down to my daughter's generation?

And it was then, still struggling for an answer yet empowered by the question, that I broke the surface.

A Letter to the Future

Dear Twyla Bella,

I write these words during a clear winter night, not long after our celebratory solstice gathering around a bonfire. A big moon shines in through my window. Her glow has always been special to us, one of the elements that define our relationship. Solstice celebrates the long nights of starlight and moonbeams, the mystery of darkness and the living things that thrive in it, from the great horned owls we used to hear when we lived in the Yukon to the phosphorescent, tiny algae that ignite the ocean night. That is a good darkness. Essential. And so is the other side of solstice: the return of longer days and all the growth, diversity and hope they bring.

I cannot contain my impulse to write down these thoughts for you. You are only three years old, yet I want you to know that I have been part of a collective effort to hand down to your generation a world worth living in. That does not mean that I am doing enough. Certainly not nearly as much as many others. But it does mean that I care and try. Those who do more give me a sense of identity when I need it most. Their work is a trigger for these words, which I hope you will read some day.

I began worrying about the impact of people on each other and the rest of the living world at a very young age, long before you were born or I had even met Gail, my fabulous wife (lucky me!) and your mother. I first wrote on these themes for my high school newspaper (I hope to find these pieces for you). Your birth, however, changed me in two ways. First, it intensified my awareness of human-caused impacts on the planet and my desire to do something about it. More importantly, whether I accepted it intellectually or not, every spiritual and emotional aspect of my being decided to believe in a long-term living planet. To believe otherwise would be unfair to you, as prophecies are often self-fulfilling. So I tried to jettison my gigantic cynicism, at least most of it most of the time, and focused on the positive and doable. As part of that commitment, I began this scrapbook account of what I was up to before you were born and as you were growing up.

It will be years before you are old enough to read and understand these words. Meanwhile, there is a fire of resistance against the deterioration of the biosphere that is burning brighter and brighter. This is also a fire of renewal, in which we humans may actually fulfill our potential to be a wise species that practises coexistence. Of course, I expect huge losses to occur. By the time you understand these words, whatever peace and coexistence we may have achieved will be fragile, subject to catastrophic upheavals and in need of further acts of resistance and renewal. What matters most is to not kill the future altogether. Thanks to you and others who inspire me, I believe that is possible.

Love,
Pops

CHAPTER 1

Storms and Stillness

Dear Twyla Bella,

Gail once told me that you have to love something before you can care enough to protect it. What she meant, I think, is held within this story.

It was early May in 1997. Gail and I were in our sea kayaks off the east shore of Yakobi Island, close to where Cross Sound meets the full force of the North Pacific Ocean, in southeast Alaska. After a whirlwind of long ferry rides, a night spent drinking beer in Juneau and a second night camping inside a dilapidated shed in the tiny community of Pelican, it felt good to be gliding on the water. We crossed Lisianski Inlet and travelled north along Yakobi's eastern shoreline. The yellow legs of wandering tattlers, wading birds on their northward migration, contrasted against dark intertidal rocks, and twelve sea otters converged at the entrance to Lisianski Strait. In the stillness, sometimes enhanced by drizzle, we sensuously followed every contour of the steep rocky shore. Snow patches, remnants from last winter, covered the shady side of beaches. A goshawk flew low beside us. Harbour porpoises swam by as we caught a lingcod for dinner. The evening was very rainy, yet our tarp—the only shelter we had brought—worked fine and we cooked the lingcod on a fire.

We slept on forest moss at the edge of a bluff overlooking the ocean, and woke to breaking skies. As we paddled west into Cross

Sound, flocks of marbled murrelets dove to feed at an eddy line of the tidal current. Glaciated mountains loomed large on the mainland to the north. At Cape Bingham, Gail caught a kelp greenling and I caught a black rockfish. From our kayaks we watched a large grizzly bear walking on the rocky beach, feeding on crabs exposed by the low tide. Like the crest of a standing wave in a tidal rip, its massive bulk rose and fell ever so slightly with each step. We landed on a sandy beach where we had intended to camp, but fresh grizzly tracks and crashing sounds emanating from the forest sent us across the water to a small rocky island where we spent the night instead. The island had fresh deer sign and wolf scats full of deer hair. When we left camp in the morning, the wind blew at about twenty knots from the northwest. Our weather radio was in a blackout zone, transporting us to a past era where marine weather forecasts did not exist. Yes, we did have a nautical chart, tide table and compass, yet we now had to make our safety decisions by observing and interpreting the clouds, winds and waves, directly, rather than listening to the radio. Turning south along the west coast of Yakobi, we were hit by swells from the west that rebounded chaotically against the cliffs. We sheltered in Surge Bay. We could not fish in these conditions; dinner was a curried dish of the seaweeds *Fucus, Ulva* and *Macrocystis*. The night was windless but with heavy downpours. The morning *seemed* still, but once we left shore the wind blew strongly from the southwest and the swell was large. The weather gods were playing a north–south tug of war and we had no forecast.

Our rhythm remained steady for the remainder of the journey: paddle when possible, shelter when slammed. Our days were punctuated by sightings of grizzly bears, swells that swallowed and spat out offshore rocks, the barnacled backs of grey whales that expanded the definition of grace. Perhaps because of these bears, swells and whales, we talked, for the first time after years of being together, about something we had never spoken of before. By the end of the trip, there was no doubt in either of our minds. We will not lose sight of what we have seen. We will invite you here, to Earth.

TWYLA BELLA, GAIL LIKES to remind me that my profession and identity are inseparable. "No way!" I attempt to deny, hoping to come across as a cooler cat than I really am. But I suppose she is right. When it comes to the blows, I am an ecologist. That has been my career and living for more than two decades. And some of it *is* the stuff of cool cats. Discovering something new about nature can be as thrilling, I imagine, as the buzz improvising musicians get when they reach new dimensions during a jam.

Yet, as an ecologist, I also know many unpleasant things about the state of the world. The words "extinction," "over-exploitation" and "climate change" pervade the scientific literature that I read routinely. I also write some of this literature. To be fair, science journals often uplift me with success stories: ecosystems restored from degradation, indigenous people co-managing large biological reserves, and evidence that people can behave in ways that reduce the greenhouse gases that are altering the climate and acidifying the oceans. But even at the best of times, consumer apathy and political inertia threaten to burst my optimism.

I did not resist that threat for a long time. During my early adult life I accepted defeat, passively, by dividing my time between some of the Earth's last wild places and an imagined variant of Ray Bradbury's fictional dystopia *Fahrenheit 451,* where the best we might do is sink while swimming towards shore.

Yet on February 27, 2004, you entered the world. Clichés abound on parenthood changing people. Who knew that some would be true.

So my letters to you began when you were three. Letters that grappled with the forces shaping the world that will be handed down to you; words you would not be able to read and understand for years to come. At first they were an attempt to reach a pact with myself that would stave off doom and gloom from our relationship, at least until you came of age. Something meant to stay between father and daughter. But in the process, I realized I could not leave it at that. My ongoing immersion in the scientific literature impressed on me that science was clear on so many issues that required immediate attention, including the economics of why it is to everyone's advantage to let go of our fossil fuel economy as soon as possible. Yet consumer behaviour and voting choices—which presumably can drive the policies that shape the fate of the biosphere and human societies—continued to lag far behind science. Scientific knowledge alone, I realized, was not about to kick-start the restructuring of society that we need so badly. So what would?

"Nothing," my rational mind answered. "Corporations focused on the bottom line, not governments representing the people, run the world…so do not even bother…just enjoy swimming towards shore." But after a particularly heated negotiation with myself, I realized that history could not be disregarded. Against unbelievable odds, regular citizens working within their democratic rights have, in many nations, fought the economic establishment and managed to abolish slavery, racism, gender inequality and other injustices, at least from a legal standpoint. These are incredible success stories. Slavery in eighteenth-century Britain played an economic role not unlike the one fossil fuels play in the current global economy. Yet both are fraught with similar ethical issues. If regular citizens could abolish British slavery nearly three centuries ago, then it is not impossible for a global democratic movement to replace the current economic system with one that values the atmosphere and ecosystems that sustain humanity. Enough of the science needed to inform and support this transition already exists. But, once again, what would it take to generate the critical mass required for change?

Dwelling on that question, I've come to believe that scientists are failing to influence a shift in the world because most of us live mainly in our heads. We usually appeal to other people's intellect, which is a sure way to disengage most non-scientists. At the same time, we cannot take science out of the picture; we would risk having only beliefs, and the economic forces at large could dismiss these all too easily. Shifting society in any meaningful way will require science and *more*. Science and *emotion*. Science and *connection* to the essence of the Earth.

So I decided to keep writing letters to you, my young daughter.

Words that reflect the sharp knife edge on which the fate of the biosphere rests. Stories that speak of the empowerment that arises when people care to protect what they truly love.

These letters, of course, are yours. Yet I also imagine sharing them with others who might be persuaded to favour a paradigm shift in the economics and politics that influence the fate of the biosphere. Those who might be moved by a synergism of science and connection—connection to the Earth of today, connection to the Earth of the future—as encapsulated by the father-daughter relationship held within these letters.

TODAY, I AM FLOODED by images of you. At three months old you laid on the moss, under the canopy of the spruce and pine forest near our home in the Yukon, arms outstretched by your head, your gaze skyward. At five months Gail held you against her belly, crossing a creek in the near-midnight sunset of southeast Alaska during summer solstice; the next day she took you inside her kayak cockpit, where you travelled together only metres from shore in a symbolic first kayak journey. At eight months I held you against my chest, Gail beside us, as we walked from our home, forded the frigid river and entered the boreal forest to pick cranberries, collect meadow mushrooms and hunt grouse. At sixteen months, in our home boreal forest, you clambered over logs, rolled in dirt, ate the bittersweet soapberries that the bears and indigenous people of this territory cherish.

And then our home shifted to southern British Columbia, just outside Vancouver. That meant letting go of northern things. Yet it also meant embracing new possibilities—among them, the escalating synergies of a global movement for action against climate change. When you were five, at the Climate Change Action Rally in downtown Vancouver, which was timed with the 2009 Copenhagen Climate Summit, you stood near the microphone as first I and then Gail spoke to the crowd of a few hundred activists. Then you had your very own impulse. You asked for the microphone to be lowered and, facing the crowd, you spoke these clear and loud words: "I hope people don't drive."

From that moment, I began to struggle with how much I should tell you about the state of the world. There is a risk to over-sheltering, yet there is also injustice in robbing you of your childhood too early. Worse. I was told the story of a depressed teen-ager who committed suicide, leaving a trail of the environmental doom-and-gloom readings that propelled him into the dark vortex. But the cat was out of the bag. That day at your first climate rally, you understood enough to sense that something serious was hap-pening, and that that something was not going to go away easily.

I CONSTANTLY THINK ABOUT how climate change is shaping the world that will be handed down to you. For most of the last fifty million years, the concentration of carbon dioxide (CO_2)—a gas that traps heat by keeping solar radiation from bouncing back to space—declined within Earth's atmosphere. And so the planet cooled, slowly and steadily, from a place once hostile to many of today's life forms to the friendlier planet that eventually allowed civilization to emerge. Yet it took people only a couple of centu-ries to turn atmospheric chemistry upside down. The discovery that we could exploit energy stored within fossil fuels unleashed the potential for great genius. And for suicide by genius. Com-bustion of fossil fuels became the new normal. The growing de-mand for raw materials led to fossil fuel-powered technologies capable of destroying forests and soils, prime natural systems for removing CO_2 from the atmosphere, faster than ever before.

I imagine the early industrialists. They stared at billowing dark clouds that emanated from their coal-burning plants, at seas of stumps that were once ancient forests, thrilled by production. Per-haps they thought of Earth's atmosphere as a boundless dump—their own actions as taking a few grains of sand from a vast des-ert. I can partly understand them. After all, they had no historical precedent or scientific analysis to foresee the consequences of their industries. But that alibi began to crumble in 1894, when Svante Ar-rhenius, a Swedish physical chemist and Nobel laureate, produced the first scientific climate model for the planet. A true prophet if there ever was one, Arrhenius showed that atmospheric CO_2 had been increasing and therefore the climate would warm. More than a century later, during which scientists have confirmed, refined and expanded Arrhenius's model, most industrialists and politicians continue to behave as if market delusions supersede physical reality. Despite scientists having mapped out a viable exit from our current path of rising emissions and imminent disaster, the fossil fuel industry and its public subsidies only get bigger every year.

As I write these words, the concentration of CO_2 in the atmosphere is 40 percent greater than the maximum level known for the eight hundred thousand years that preceded the industrial revolution, and rising. The last time Earth's atmosphere sustained a level of carbon dioxide as high as today's was fifteen to twenty million years ago. Back then, global temperatures were three to six degrees Celsius warmer, polar ice caps did not exist, and sea levels were twenty-five to forty metres above present levels. The Earth's paleoclimatic history is warning us of the potential for dark times ahead. Yet we can see this approaching darkness only because light still exists.

AND WE LOVE A good storm only because stillness remains possible. To show you what I mean, I will tell you the story of when you began to handle your own sea kayak. I will never forget that first paddle, when you were seven years old. It was a very cold and gloomy day in late December. The pouring rain blew horizontally while wind gusts swept spray from the top of whitecaps. We had just bought you your first, second-hand kayak, and in your excitement you just *had* to use it that very same day. We dressed with every possible thermal and waterproof layer and launched our boats inside a bay, within the extra protection of a breakwater. Heads down, rain needles thrown against our squinting eyes, we paddled into the wind for short bursts, then drifted back during moments of exhaustion, repeating the process over and over. Twyla Storm.

Towards the end of that winter, after your eighth birthday, we paddled together, each in our own boat, near Hutt Island, close to our Bowen Island home. The tide was very low. Snow flurries swept the horizon, fleetingly lit when clouds cracked just enough for light to burst through. On a rocky islet, double-crested and pelagic cormorants stood with wings outstretched, their feathers glowing iridescent blue. Oystercatchers ran on the same rock, just above the water, their brightly orange beaks ignited by the streaming sunlight, their plumage a deep black. We pulled up the crab trap, you doing most of the work; no luck this time. Just as the wind started to pick up, we landed on the beach, lay on the moss and hid inside the forest until a lull in the storm lured us back to the water. But the calm did not last. A squall suddenly picked up, blowing hard against the tide as we worked our way around a cliff that dropped vertically into the chop. "Can I take a rest?" you asked. "Twyla Bella," I replied, "being on the ocean means that there are times when you cannot rest." You offered no response. You just paddled harder.

THIS SHARING OF WIND and sea was unfolding against a scary background. Canada's Conservative government, with Prime Minister Stephen Harper at the helm, had been waging war against your future: dismantling environmental legislation, muzzling federal scientists and eliminating government programs aimed at the scientific management of natural resources. Their anti-science stance unabashedly aimed to accelerate the exploitation of bitumen—a very dirty fossil fuel—from Alberta's tar sands (also known as oil sands) and fast-track the approval of the proposed Northern Gateway Pipeline, which, if built, would transport that bitumen to the coast of British Columbia to be exported via supertankers to China.

The week before our paddle, on March 10, 2012, I delivered a letter in person to our Conservative member of parliament, John Weston. In it I described a study, just published in *Nature Climate Change*, by University of Victoria's Neil Swart and Andrew Weaver. These climatologists estimate that the burning of all proven reserves of fossil fuels—those reserves that can be extracted economically today—would raise global temperatures by 1.35 degrees Celsius. That may not sound like a lot, but it is. Humanity's appetite for fossil fuels has caused Earth to warm 0.8 degrees in the last hundred years, which is already too much—we can see that in the increasing frequency of droughts and severe storms. An additional 1.35 degrees would create a world more than two degrees warmer than in pre-industrial times, pushing the planet into the perilous zone of rising sea levels and other extreme conditions that could destabilize civilization.

The scary part is the 1.35-degree estimate is a best-case scenario. When fossil fuel reserves that are uneconomical to extract today are added to the calculations, the figure jumps to nine degrees, at minimum. This scenario is not impossible because today's ugly toad could become tomorrow's Prince Charming. To show you what I mean, let's look at the history of the tar sands. Alberta's bitumen reserves became known to industrialists in the late nineteenth century, but were regarded as unworthy—too dirty and difficult to extract—for nearly a hundred years. So nobody cared to dig them up. That began to change in the late twentieth century, when the 1973 embargo by the Organization of Arab Petroleum Exporting Countries and the concurrent dwindling of conventional oil supplies elevated the tar sands to economic darling. By the early 2000s, corporate giants were rushing to exploit them. By 2011, when Harper established his majority government, the bursts of money exploding from the tar sands had become so powerful that no other ecological or economic consideration could compete. Under the new power of the tar sands, everything that had once defined Canada as a nation of good global citizens began to crumble. Don't ever let anybody tell you that reserves that are too difficult to extract today will stay in the ground indefinitely.

Now let's imagine that the fossil fuel lobby musters some minimal mercy on the planet and decides to extract only the stuff that is relatively cheap and easy to get today. Would a 1.35-degree temperature rise still be a best-case scenario? To come up with the answer, first consider "positive feedback loops"—indirect mechanisms in which relatively small temperature rises initiate other processes that create yet more heat. For instance, warming in the Arctic and Subarctic has already reduced the area covered by summer sea ice and begun to melt the permafrost. As a consequence, solar radiation that would have been reflected back into space by white sea ice is now being absorbed by dark unfrozen ocean, and the melting permafrost is releasing greenhouse gases that had been stored frozen underground. Both of these mechanisms exacerbate global warming. Next, consider the fact that bitumen extraction destroys peat wetlands, which also store greenhouse gases underground. As giant machines rip apart these landscapes, they release vast quantities of sequestered carbon into the atmosphere, further increasing the climate impacts of the tar sands. You've probably guessed where I am going with this. The 1.35-degree estimate does not account for positive feedback loops or the destruction of peat wetlands. On top of that, Swart and Weaver's calculations exclude the amount of CO_2 generated during extraction—which is greater for tar sands than for conventional fossil fuels—and therefore underestimate tar sand emissions by about 17 percent.

Clearly, the 1.35-degree rise remains a best-case scenario. But it is a very useful one, to be sure. Good scientific models distill particular drivers of change, and that is exactly what Swart and Weaver's study does. It helps us understand the *relative* contribution of different fossil fuels to the global warming that could occur if business as usual continues, which is why I felt compelled to meet with Weston.

Of the warming that would result from burning all proven reserves of fossil fuels, coal would bear the lion's share (68 percent) while the contribution of Alberta's tar sands would be only 2 percent. This is a clear indication that policy-makers and activists should pay closer attention to coal; no arguments there. The concern that I shared with many others was that Canada's Conservative government was likely to spin the study into a victory that justified even faster development of the tar sands—something the mainstream media was already cheering on: "Coal, not oil sands, the true climate change bad guy, analysis shows" (*The Globe and Mail* and *Winnipeg Free Press*); "Coal, not oil sands, causes global warming: study" (*CTV*); "Coal, not oil sands, the real threat to climate, study finds" (*Toronto Star*).

The faulty logic of those headlines was easy to spot. No country is about to grant Canada a monopoly for exploiting the tar sands while leaving its own fossil fuels and money in the ground. Keeping warming below two degrees requires that all nations work together to concurrently phase out fossil fuel production. The exploitation of Alberta's tar sands, therefore, is inseparable from broader issues of equity. Canadians represent half a percent of the global population. According to calculations by Neil Swart, if everyone in the world developed their resources and produced emissions at the same per capita rate as Canada, the global temperature would go way beyond the two-degree threshold within a few decades. The logical conclusion of Swart and Weaver's study, therefore, is that consumption of coal *and* tar sands *and* gas *and* conventional oil must all be phased out as soon as possible. Many other climatologists have arrived at the same conclusion by way of different case studies.

By the time I met with Weston, Prime Minister Harper had been advertising, loud and clear, that acknowledging scientific evidence was not in his agenda. In fact, the extent to which his government had been publicly scoffing at international cooperation to mitigate climate change was nothing short of embarrassing to anyone who cares about Canada's role in the world. (As Mark Twain said: "Loyalty to the country always. Loyalty to the government when it deserves it.") Only two months before our wintry kayak adventure, Canada's Minister of the Environment, Peter Kent, had delivered a speech to the Calgary Chamber of Commerce, an urban epicentre for tar sands development, in which he stated:

> I'm here today to explain to you how and why Environment Canada is a strategic partner to everyone in this room…everyone who does business in Calgary, in Alberta, in Canada.
>
> I'm not here to kill your buzz. I'm here to generate buzz of a different sort…
>
> Let me explain.
>
> In the year since I became Environment Minister, we've reviewed and renewed our approach as a

government department: we are still environmental regulators, but we better understand what we need to do to enhance our efficiency—and yours.

Later in the speech, with unparalleled charm, Kent delivered his punchline.

Coming out of the United Nations climate change conference in Durban last month, my early Christmas present to myself—and to Canada—was to exercise our legal right to get out of the Kyoto Protocol which, with all its deficiencies, did not work for Canada.

Sitting in Weston's office, I was aware that the letter I had brought was my tenth one to government that year—one of hundreds I had written during my adult life—and that this was my second meeting with my member of parliament that year. He listened attentively and nodded politely while I explained the content of my letter. When I was done, he thanked me for my engagement in democracy and, mustering a look of concern, offered to help create opportunities for cabinet ministers to listen directly to climate scientists. It was all very predictable. The illusion of being all ears was his party's cheap concession to democracy; it did not require actually doing something to slow down the growth of the fossil fuel industry. As I was leaving, I almost asked Weston if he would sponsor a private member's bill on intergenerational justice, but I figured that the joke would be wasted on him.

TWYLA BELLA, MY ATTEMPTS to do something about the climate crisis remind me of what you sensed that day at your first rally: something serious is happening, and that something is not going to go away easily. So I am drawn back to the image of you in your kayak during that winter day near Hutt Island. Snow flurries sweeping the horizon, snow-capped mountains temporarily swallowed by dark clouds, then pulled back out into the pouring

sunbeams: a sky painting of possibilities. Amidst this intense dyna-
mism of the atmosphere, the squall and tide are against you. Tired
as you are, you paddle harder.

Love,
Pops

Chapter 2

Vanishing Glimpses

Dear Twyla Bella,

My parents shaped my love for the natural world. They raised me and my siblings in Mexico City, where they infused in us a curiosity about nature through books, stories and outings into the forest fragments that surrounded that megacity. And my parents loved Mexico. Passionately. So most family vacations were spent visiting jungles, deserts, coasts and indigenous cultures farther from the city.

But not all was good. During those early years in the 1970s and early 1980s, I watched my favourite wooded haunts in the outskirts of Mexico City disappear under the pavement of suburbs. I saw remote fishing villages, where we had once been among the few white visitors, transform into international mega-resorts. I became aware that the coral reefs where we snorkelled were declining into overfished shadows of their old selves. The notions of habitat loss and extinction began to take hold in my brain.

I also watched indigenous children only a few years younger than me sleeping on the dirty pavement of traffic dividers—their parents begging for coins while the motorized chaos of Mexico City engulfed them like the torrent of development that had drowned their ancestral land. Although I could not articulate it yet, the connection between a healthy biosphere and a just society began to enter my consciousness.

Shortly after I finished high school in 1983, our family moved to British Columbia, where I embraced coastal mountains and the North Pacific Ocean as my new home. It was there that I began to study ecology.

While the natural world has always been inherent to my being, at times I have felt that my pursuit of ecology is some form of self-imposed torture. Math, an essential tool for the discipline, has been my frequent nemesis. For years I tried to flee from the scientific study of nature, unsuccessfully. Perhaps I stuck with it thanks to mentors who mustered gargantuan patience and led me through the challenges, some more gently than others. Back in April of 2003, I had my first face-to-face meeting with Colin Clark, the great mathematician at the University of British Columbia. Colin had just reviewed my equations describing a theoretical model of ecological processes that was to be part of my dissertation. As soon as I walked into his office, he asked me to sit down. He then read aloud, with the stern voice professors reserve for such occasions, the incisive words he had penned at the back of my manuscript: "THIS LOOKS LIKE A DOOMED PROJECT right now. Bush may have a better hope in Iraq than you have of completing this, this way!" Of course I was sweating but, thanks to his final words—"this way!"—I knew that what Colin really meant was that I would do much better if only I could see the forest for the trees. Still, if there ever was a cue that ecology and I should no longer be together, this was the one.

So I tried to run. But my feet were frozen. Call it lack of imagination, being chicken shit, pre-determined destiny, whatever you like. Instead of bolting I started to plot my progress against the failures of George W. Bush in Iraq. Miraculously, and not without a good dose of angst, within a couple of years I started publishing numerous mathematical models of ecological processes. In 2006, moments after I finished the oral defence of my dissertation, Gail came to me in that drab hallway of Simon Fraser University and said, "If you hit your head against the wall enough times, the wall will break." By the time the examining committee finished its deliberations and emerged to congratulate me, I understood that my commitment to ecology had been sealed, not in that moment but nearly two decades earlier, in subantarctic Chile.

IT WAS THE AUSTRAL autumn of 1989. I was gliding in my kayak, surrounded by tidal glaciers, alone in the channels of Tierra del Fuego. I came here because I wanted a glimpse of my non-human kin and origins.

I watched the vertical granite face of Cerro Yagán appear through a gap in the clouds. The mountain is namesake to a culture that coexisted for eons with the forest and the sea. That culture is dead. Yagán Indians, the original inhabitants of the Beagle Channel and Cape Horn Islands of southernmost Tierra del Fuego, no longer paddle their canoes hunting sea lions. They no longer gather chaura berries in the forest. Those not killed by European settlers quietly wasted away in Christian missions. Lakutaia Le Kipa, the last member of the Yagán race, died in 1983. In her own words, "[Yagáns] stopped wandering naked and obtaining their own food and got sick. Civilization attacked their lungs and stomach and they began to die."

Cerro Yagán dissolved into mist. Like the Yagán people, it became dark nothingness. This reminder of cultural demise contrasted with the wild vitality that still rules this part of the world. Earlier in the journey I had watched a Magellanic penguin gasp at the water surface, staining a kelp bed with its blood, while a southern sea lion bull—eager to continue the meal I had interrupted—snarled by my bow. A blasting gale had caught me during a major crossing. It made me paddle like hell. It made me wonder whether I would ever touch shore again. Soaked and glowing, my aching muscles had collapsed on the sand. I awoke from that deep slumber to the sight of Peale's dolphins propelling their bodies out of the ocean and into the air, liquid curtains dripping off their tails and bellies.

Perhaps my journey, after all, was meant to highlight the living. Paddling on I noticed a leopard seal sleeping on an iceberg. I drifted until my kayak bow touched its haul-out. The voracious, four-metre-long giant that swallows penguins whole was not aggressive with me. For a moment, it gave me a deep stare; then it closed its eyes again.

While I paddled away from the seal, a small wooden boat roared across an ice-free section of the fjord and cut towards me. It was two fishermen from Punta Arenas, a small city about two hundred kilometres to the northwest. With the extinction of Yagán culture, commercial fishermen remain among the few people whose lives are still intertwined with the fjords and channels of Tierra del Fuego. I was familiar with their company; several storms had washed me up onto their decks, where I had been received with hot food and conversation. The fishermen pulled over and invited me aboard. Of course I accepted.

Later that day, after a delightful tour of the bay, I found myself beneath the icebergs. Wearing an old wetsuit and breathing air from a rudimentary compressor, I watched men from other boats collect scallops. I marvelled at their skill for gathering their quarry, arms fluttering from the sea floor to their collecting basket with the wing-speed of cormorants diving after fish. These were the same men who overfished the seas, who illegally used dolphins and penguins as crab bait and who killed sea lions to traffic the animals' penises for Chinese aphrodisiacs. While underwater and linked to the atmosphere by an aging rubber hose, it occurred to me that my friends up on the boat likely engaged in all of these activities. Yet sharing their rim world, how could I possibly blame poor people for trying to make a living?

My camp that evening was inside a forest of southern beeches, where I saw a Magellanic woodpecker thrust its beak into the rotting wood of a coigüe tree. Its intensely red head sped back and forth in the forest shadows, a torch dancing in darkness. Back on the mainland across from Tierra del Fuego, I had seen cows grazing among the charred stumps that extend from the hilltops to the shores of the Strait of Magellan. During the 1940s and '50s settlers burned thousands of square kilometres. I lay on the moss, knowing that multinational corporations were already logging nearby, wreaking incalculable havoc on the least studied of the world's temperate forests.

When I woke up the next day the woodpecker was nowhere to be heard. In the silence I gathered red chaura berries. On the understory of succulent herbs I came upon a cormorant skeleton, abandoned by a hawk. As I stared into the bloody remains, extinct Yagáns and endangered forests weighed me down. This heaviness was not what I had come looking for. Yet, for better or for worse, it set the course for the rest of my life.

THE FOLLOWING SPRING FOUND me in Puerto Edén, a village accessible only by water, to the northwest of Punta Arenas. It was there that I met Twackol, one of the last Kaweshkar Indians, the original inhabitants of southern Chile's archipelago north of the Beagle Channel. Twackol spoke of how Kaweshkars once paddled dugout canoes to hunt sea lions. They also hunted huemul, the deer they knew as *yektal, yawurston* or *yaukhartchez*. Twackol's voice was soft and sombre. The impacts of European colonialism had destroyed his people's vision of the world and their hunting traditions. Although they outlived the Yagáns, only a handful of Kaweshkars survived; there would be no next generation.

The deer that Twackol described had become my reason for being there. Huemul are a species unique to southern Chile and Argentina. Amazing mountain climbers, they are stockier and slightly smaller than mule and black-tailed deer, their closest North American relatives. And they are endangered. Although Chilean law has long protected them from hunting, by the mid-1900s the excesses of poaching, logging and ranching had diminished huemul numbers throughout most of their formerly vast range. Before European colonization, huemul may have been most abundant in south-central Chile, where the climate is relatively benign and native vegetation once dominated the landscape. Today, most surviving animals are found at the edge of the large icecap at the heart of Twackol's territory. They have become a deer of storm and ice only because their last stronghold is too harsh and remote for most human exploitation.

And this is where I fitted in. I was among the few students of ecology (at the time, between my undergraduate and master's degrees) willing to chase ghosts in wet and cold subantarctic Chile. Inspired by my kayak trip in Tierra del Fuego, I had talked myself into believing that this was my calling. After a three-month hiatus back home in Canada—where I had enlisted the mentorship of forest ecologists and wildlife biologists and secured modest research grants from conservation organizations—I had returned to Chile for a quixotic attempt to learn something new about huemul. And the journey that had landed me in Puerto Edén had been a long one.

Three months earlier, in the dead of the austral winter of 1990, my brother Leonardo and I had left the village of Puerto Natales aboard a small fishing vessel. I wanted to study huemul during the winter because logging for the Japanese market was already underway in the vicinity of Punta Arenas, and assessing old-growth forests as potential winter habitat was a priority. The coasts of southern Chile and Alaska are the highest latitudes where temperate rainforests are found. The rainforests in both regions are fragmented by icecaps, bogs and other treeless habitats. They evolved in a cool and wet climate and have been shaped by the catastrophic disturbances of heavy winds, landslides and glacial advances, rather than by the fires of drier forests. Thus, despite their different tree species—mainly conifers in the north, evergreen hardwoods in the south—the rainforests of Alaska and southern Chile have similar ecological dynamics. The similarity was recognized by one of my mentors—ecologist Paul Alaback, then at the Forestry Sciences Laboratory in Juneau, Alaska—and was important for predicting habitat use during winter by deer, which was well known for black-tailed deer in Alaska but unstudied for huemul. When deep snow accumulates at low elevation for long periods, black-tailed deer avoid population crashes by moving into old-growth forests. These forests are a mosaic of closed-canopy areas, where very large trees intercept snow and provide shelter, broken by openings where strong winds have knocked down dead or dying trees and sunlight can pour in, boosting the productivity of understory food plants during the growing season.

Brimming with youthful over-enthusiasm, Leonardo and I had hopped aboard the first fishing boat to leave the village, in spite of the fishermen's warning that they were not travelling to the most remote areas where huemul abound. On our departure day, it was sleeting and the seas were rough. Leonardo and I crammed into the tiny boat cabin with the crew of four Natalinos and sought warmth from the rusty woodstove. The stove stood only a few feet from the engine, a loud and productive source of noxious fumes. Though challenging from the start, the situation was manageable until the crew started smoking cigarettes and frying a chunk of dead cow. Leonardo, my strong-stomached brother, remained calm. Not I. Within seconds I was out in the sleet, my face being washed by waves crashing over the deck, releasing my stomach content into the Golfo Jorge Montt. This was a skill I had developed during earlier boat rides in Tierra del Fuego and was able to use in subsequent trips.

Sleet turned into snow. The atmosphere was so gloomy that midday felt like dusk. "Quick stops" to visit other fishermen we encountered along the way turned into hours of storytelling about poaching huemul and surviving knife fights.

Having covered sixty nautical miles in sixty hours, Leonardo and I were excited to be dropped off at a bay where we might find huemul. Immediately we came upon their droppings and soon found various sets of fresh tracks. Yet, true to the fishermen's warning, a family that had tried to homestead in that area had done its share of forest-burning and venison-eating. For ten days Leonardo and I camped on the snow-covered shore and followed huemul tracks without ever catching a glimpse of the mythical creatures.

I decided to count my losses and look for a different study site, which only led to other false starts. Leonardo returned home. My friend John Townley arrived soon after, only to spend his first few weeks immersed in fruitless, wet bushwhacks. Eventually, someone in Punta Arenas took pity on us and said, "Ve a Puerto Edén y los encontrarás" ("Go to Puerto Edén and you will find them").

Once in Puerto Edén, I met the old man known as Guachi-pato. With an ever-present cigarette hanging from a corner of his mouth, Guachipato was a pirate of sorts and the godfather of all huemul poachers. Born in central Chile of European descent, he came to Puerto Edén in the 1950s. He soon developed a respectful relationship with Kaweshkar elders, who taught him the ways of the huemul. Before boat engines became available to him in the 1970s, he had travelled much of the coast by sail and oar, camping in myriad coves along the way. Deep wrinkles in his weathered face mapped his long journeys through the archipelago. Guachi-pato was charmingly intimidating: "Si te comes uno de mis chivos te corto el cógote!" ("If you eat one of my goats [as he referred to huemul], I will chop your head off!"). These were the very first words Guachipato uttered to me. He then exploded into laughter and showed me the head of a freshly killed huemul.

It was a challenge to win Guachipato's trust. But subantarctic Chile had taught me patience, and time was on my side. Eventu-ally, after many visits and countless rounds of yerba mate—the bitter South American tea that is imbibed from a gourd—Guachi-pato came up with the goods; he took my chart and pointed to the best spot for studying the deer.

A FEW DAYS AFTER my last audience with Guachipato, one of the storms that almost continuously batter the archipelago died down. The wind hushed. Reflections of blue sky oscillated on the ripples of a silk-like sea. Deep inside the remoteness of this coast, John Townley and I kayaked into the long and narrow fjord where Guachipato had sent us. Knowing that the benign weather would be short-lived, I revelled in the sunshine that glis-tened on the fjord's granite walls. Yet part of me was burnt out, tired of stalking ghosts, and cynically wondering whether I was about to become the butt of one of Guachipato's jokes.

Gliding among icebergs, we came upon the huge wall of a tidal glacier. Across the bay, we set up camp where a broad valley met the shore. Although we did not know it at the time, this gla-cier and the valley at its foot would be our home and backyard for the next two and half months. And we were to share it with huemul.

It did not take long before we started meeting the deer. Initially they were skittish, allowing only fleeting encounters, but within a couple of days they got used to our presence. I will never forget my first close look. Two males lay down near each other by a lake near our camp; the sun, briefly filtering between clouds, backlit the velvet that covered their antlers. Across the lake at the base of a rocky ridge, two females—an adult and a yearling—fed side by side. This early in the spring the deer were still wearing dense winter coats. Glowing golden in the sunlight, their coarse hairs seemed to radiate incandescent warmth.

As spring advanced, we observed the deer emerge from the orange brightness of moss-covered cliffs and bound across grassland—their hooves splashing in shallow pools—and pause silhouetted against walls of ice. We could soon recognize twenty-two individuals by the shapes of their coat markings and antlers, and began to learn the stories that made up their lives: the plants they ate, the bluffs they climbed to give birth out of the reach of predators like culpeo foxes, the spectacular sparring matches in which males clashed antlers.

Using techniques developed for the study of black-tailed deer by one of my mentors—Matt Kirchhoff with the Alaska Department of Fish and Game—I measured a high density of huemul scats in the old-growth forests that rimmed the grassland. These data suggested that the deer had spent much of the previous winter in this forest. The similarity to Matt's findings for black-tailed deer in Alaska supported the idea that the mix of closed canopy shelter and food-rich openings provided by old-growth forests were important for huemul, and that logging plans in southern Chile needed to consider impacts on the deer.

Eventually, John and I ran out of food. A venison meal would be a tad inconsistent with our research objectives, and the fjord's low salinity meant there were no shellfish to forage on. With only wild berries left to eat, we had to kayak back to Puerto Edén. This took us two and half stormy days. For much of the journey squalls swept the channels, enveloping us in blinding whirlwinds of spray and thrusting needle-like rain against our faces. As large waves broke below a stretch of cliffs, John capsized into the freezing water. Calmly, he managed to re-enter his kayak. Cold and hungry but alive and well, we paddled on.

TWYLA BELLA, FIVE YEARS elapsed before I returned to Chile. In the interim, I published a scientific paper (my first!) on huemul, completed studies on Dall's sheep of the Yukon (the research for my master's degree) and, to top it all, met and married your mother, Gail.

During those years, I pondered many questions posed by my initial encounters with huemul. Eventually, research grants provided the opportunity to return to my old study site and attempt to find some answers. Surely, my experience of living amidst a pristine huemul population was about to replay itself, right?

But my return to Chile in 1995 was to a vastly different scene. Stopping in Puerto Edén, I was delighted to find Guachipato still alive. Raconteur extraordinaire, icon of knowledge and dark humour accumulated through more than forty years of living on this isolated archipelago, Guachipato made me laugh as he told stories and extracted my gossip from the last five years. Then he dropped a bomb. In 1991, Guachipato told me, a local villager had introduced eighteen head of cattle into the study site. I was speechless. I had assumed, naively, that this rugged fjord at the edge of the continental ice cap would remain free of cattle.

A few days later, my research crew—Paulo Corti from Chile and Jasper Stephens from Canada—and I crammed into the small fishing vessel *Lorena*. Our captain and crew consisted of two Puerto Edén residents, Victor Oswaldo Muñoz and Victor Manuel Zuñiga. As we travelled towards the fjord where I had studied huemul, I was amused by the irony that *Lorena* and "The Victors" had been the ones hired in 1991 to transport the cattle to my original study site. The nature of the journey was predictable. For forty-eight nautical miles we chugged along, slowly navigating in full storm conditions, pumping out the steadily flooding hull and watching

Victor Oswaldo alternate repairs between two moody engines.

Once at the study site, it did not take long before I confronted evidence of change. Where I had camped before, watching huemul sniff my tent and eye me with curiosity, there were countless piles of cow dung. Where John Townley and I had watched sparring matches between bucks, now stood an empty corral. The cattle people, our hosts *in absentia*, had left behind a tin shack with a rusty wood stove. For this we were grateful, as we hastily brought in our gear and sought shelter from the storm. Later that day we took a census of the livestock on the grassland that the huemul had been using in 1990. We counted twenty head of cattle, including four young calves, and found two skeletons. The cattle had trampled much of the vegetation in the open habitats where huemul had fed five years before during my previous visit. We sighted two huemul bucks on a slope about four hundred metres away, but they bolted over a ridge as soon as they saw us.

For five days the storm continued. We lived cloaked in an ominous atmosphere. The wind was relentless. A nearby waterfall roared, swollen with rain. Ice collapsing from the glacier into the sea thundered. The heavy hooves of cattle eroding the earth echoed through my brain. I felt haunted by the ghosts of deer.

Yet our fieldwork progressed. It became clear that cattle foraged only on the grassland at the valley bottom, leaving other habitats undisturbed. As suggested by the relatively high density of their scats, huemul had made heavy use of the old-growth forest during the previous winter. We also observed five skittish huemul on the bluffs. Although the cattle and an increase in poaching had combined to drive deer numbers down, there were still some huemul in the area.

On the sixth day, the first windless morning since our arrival, I decided to move on. The Victors rowed the *Lorena* (which had been named after Victor Manuel's daughter) through dense icebergs before starting the engines. It wasn't long before we had to pump the flooding hull and repair the engines. But this time we were heading towards a pristine fjord recommended by Guachipato. Suddenly, the sky brightened. Peale's dolphins darted

across our bow. Southern sea lions and Magellanic penguins sur-
faced nearby. All good omens.

At twilight, we arrived at our new site and found huemul on
the beach. Guachipato had provided us with another treasure. We
stayed for three weeks, studying fifty-nine different deer that we
could identify by natural markings, our spirits soaring as we lived
among some of the last members of an endangered species.

TWYLA BELLA, IN THOSE fjords I began to understand that I belong
to a generation that is both privileged and cursed. Privileged because we still have the option, limited though it is, of experiencing
large ecosystems that maintain their vibrancy. Cursed because we
know that those ecosystems, and the myriad species they support,
are vanishing at dizzying rates.

I never returned to Twackol's territory to search for huemul. Instead, I pursued more advanced studies in ecology and
reshaped my personal vision about how my work should address
the ongoing biodiversity crisis. Huemul still deserved the attention
of conservation biologists; that was a given. Yet Chileans I had
worked with were capable of getting the job done. For example,
Paulo Corti has completed doctoral studies on huemul and made
important contributions to the conservation genetics of the species. Guachipato's sons, who helped me access the first study site
in 1990, traded their poaching lifestyle for jobs as park wardens
responsible for protecting huemul; their anti-poaching patrols
supported a collaborative effort between conservationists and the
Chilean government, which removed cattle from my former study
site in 2004. Since then, studies by Chilean scientists suggest that
huemul may be rebuilding their numbers in the area. Clearly, the
show could go on, and did go on, without me.

So I began to study other species, focusing on how the vibrant tension between predators and prey—and the loss of that
tension—affects ecosystems. Soon I will tell you more about those
journeys for which that drab hallway at Simon Fraser University
was a mere stop along the way. Journeys that originate, at least
in part, in the channels and fjords of southern Chile, where I

learned to cover distance—through space, time and possibility.

Back in 1990, after months of hiding from sleet squalls and living in the fjord with huemul and without communication to the outside world (satellite phones were unheard of at that time), John Townley and I blurred the boundary between ourselves and our Cro-Magnon ancestors. Barefoot in the drizzle, we squatted beside a fire, a tiny glow in the fog that we fuelled with the wooden debris of a past avalanche. In my hand I held an antler cast off years before by a huemul buck. I had found it lying on the moss, in a tiny valley tucked between cliffs and an ocean of ice. An infinite number of snowflakes and countless more raindrops had touched that antler. A faint growth of algae had greened some of its whiteness. I imagined the surrounding mountain range and ice-cap mapped on this biforked, sharply pointed, piece of bone. Reflected on the antler's surface, I envisioned glimpses into the lives of huemul. The images were not unlike those held by traditional hunter-gatherers and symbolized the large ecosystems that we may still be able to conserve.

Love,
Pops

CHAPTER 3

Vibrant Tension

Dear Twyla Bella,

I first read *The King's Stilts* aloud to you when you were three—and I nearly freaked. It all started innocently enough. I had borrowed the book from our local library, a routine step in my attempts to satisfy your thirst for stories. But once we were snuggled up for bedtime reading, my jaw dropped lower and lower as the narrative unfolded. Written in 1939 by Dr. Seuss, *The King's Stilts* turned out to be a treatise on how behavioural interactions between species can affect the fate of ecosystems. Dr. Seuss, I realized with a tinge of envy, had scooped ecologists by nearly fifty years in describing some fundamental ways of nature.

This is how the story goes. The Kingdom of Binn is far below sea level and surrounded by potentially threatening waters. Dike Trees provide a critical ecosystem service; their roots stabilize a barrier that keeps the ocean from pouring into the kingdom. But these roots are also food to Nizzards, large crow-like birds. If Nizzards, herbivores in the middle of the food chain, were to be left unchecked, Dike Trees would go extinct, the sea would pour in, and the Kingdom of Binn would drown.

But Binn also has Patrol Cats, top predators that scare Nizzards away from Dike Trees. Patrol Cats need not kill to perform their ecological role; the mere presence of these fearsome predators makes Nizzards more cautious and spend less time feeding on roots, indirectly allowing life in the kingdom to persist.

Human folly soon enters the scene. Through a crazy Seussian plot, Patrol Cats fall into disarray, Nizzards are released from the threat of Patrol Cats, Dike Trees decline and the kingdom of Binn faces imminent collapse. A struggle ensues to undo the mess. A grim end appears inevitable until, in the nick of time, human wisdom restores the ecological role of Patrol Cats and the Kingdom of Binn is saved.

THE KING'S STILTS **IS** an abstract model of what I call vibrant tension: the ecological effect that predators have, not by killing individual prey animals one at a time, but rather by scaring entire prey populations into behaviours—such as hiding and vigilance—that save prey from being eaten. But at a cost. The more prey avoid danger, the less they can feed, which slows down growth and hinders reproduction, the ultimate driver of their existence. Yet death by predation terminates both growth and reproduction, abruptly. Drives and dangers push and pull. They determine where and when grazers choose to graze and mesopredators (mid-level predators) venture to consume smaller prey. They build tension and define that quasi-Shakespearean dilemma of animal life: "To feed or to hide now: what will give me the most descendants over my lifetime?" The prey's moment-by-moment responses to that dilemma shape the very nature of ecosystems.

Here is a classic example. On meadows where spiders live in the understory, grasshoppers, the spider's prey, feed on poor-quality foods on the canopy. When spiders are removed experimentally, grasshoppers move down to the understory, where they feast on more nutritious herbs. This result may seem simple, but in fact it is rather profound. It shows that predation risk from spiders, or its absence, redistributes in space the impacts of grasshopper herbivory on plants, which ultimately affects plant diversity, canopy structure, soil chemistry, rates of litter decomposition and so forth. Pretty much what went on between Patrol Cats, Nizzards and Dike Trees. Which gives ecologists a good starting point for thinking about the state of the planet because, almost everywhere, humans are stripping ecosystems of their vibrancy by diminishing top predators. And the oceans, where most fisheries target the largest predatory fish, are no exception.

TWYLA BELLA, CLOSE YOUR eyes and imagine our home coast of British Columbia before European colonization. Back then, fishing at sea was not something that just happened. Only after creating a bond with materials from the forest and the kelp beds would fishers earn the privilege of catching big predatory fish like halibut, lingcod and sablefish. Giant red cedars had to be felled through controlled burning. Logs had to be floated out on rivers from the forest to the seashore, where carvers shaped them into canoes. Hooks had to be made from bones, the hard wood of oceanspray or knots in the wood of fir and hemlock trees. The stipes (the equivalent of stems) of bull kelp had to be collected, cured and joined into longlines. Yellow cedar slabs had to be carved into paddles. None of this happened quickly. Everyone had time to remember the respect and responsibilities that fishing entailed.

Now, open your eyes and see the world as it is today. Plastic credit cards are just about the only credentials you need to back your SUV and trailer down a concrete ramp, release your aluminum skiff onto the water, rev up your Japanese engine, turn on your made-in-China GPS unit and fish finder, and, voila! Let's go hammer some fish!

Okay, I admit it. That last paragraph was the classic "Alejandro rant" that drives you and Gail crazy. Overly zealous and more than a tad disingenuous. After all, we and most of our friends are far from saintly. We *love* to roar around in skiffs and pull up dinner.

Still, my point remains. Slow is gone. So is small.

On top of the damage inflicted by us sport fishers, industrial fleets have been decimating populations of predatory fish within a couple decades from the opening of a fishery. These fleets deplete nearby areas first and then fish farther and farther from port to the point that, by the year 2000, their collective rates of fuel consumption and greenhouse gas emissions equalled those of the Netherlands. All in the pursuit of lower and lower earnings. The low-hanging fruit is long gone, so most industrial fisheries have become a bad joke kept afloat by perverse government subsidies. And the industry keeps sinking lower and lower, depleting fish from deeper layer after deeper layer.

And some types of aquaculture exacerbate the problem. Take salmon farms on the coast of British Columbia, which consume vast amounts of Chilean whiting, mackerel and anchovies. These forage fish should have directly fed people, as well as whales, sea birds and wild predatory fish, but instead are shipped, with tremendous fossil fuel consumption, from the southern to the northern hemisphere to raise salmon crowded into net pens. And salmon farms can, in some cases, be epicentres of pollution and disease that potentially contribute to the decline of wild salmon.

I know...I know...my name is Alejandro Frid and I am a nihilist...breathe...

IT IS JULY 2009, near the end of a three-week research trip with my friend and colleague Anne Salomon, an assistant professor at Simon Fraser University. With her graduate students and other team members, we have been working along the southeast coast of Haida Gwaii, a remote archipelago in northern British Columbia. That afternoon, I am still buzzing with the energy of having walked, only hours ago, amidst the ancient Sitka spruces and red cedars of Windy Bay where, twenty years before, members of the Haida Nation blockaded logging operations. That courageous act of civil disobedience, in which dozens of elders and young people were arrested, led to the protection of what is now the vast Gwaii Haanas National Park Reserve and Haida Heritage Site.

The ocean is calm as we roar on the skiff, piloted by Leandre Vigneault, who was born and raised on these islands. Rowan Trebilco, a Ph.D. candidate in Anne's lab, is with us. When we arrive at our destination—an offshore pinnacle near the Tar Islands— the tidal current stretches the long fronds of bull kelp horizontally. After donning dry suits and scuba gear, Rowan and I plunge into the clear water as Leandre avoids miring the engine in the swirling kelp. We enter clouds of black and yellowtail rockfish. Sunlight streams through the kelp forest, yet there is no time to enjoy the view. We must drop below the surface current before being swept off the underwater pinnacle. So we plummet past the long stipes of kelp and along the rock wall to a depth of thirty metres. The current is slower here, but only somewhat. Plumose anemones, their stubby bodies bent by the tidal flow, form a dwarf forest of whiteness on the dark rocky wall.

We settle into our task of surveying fish and the results are mind-blowing. Two huge lingcod, the top predatory fish of rocky reefs in this coast, sit on the bottom near each other. Peering down, we see two large red-orange fish. They are yelloweye rockfish, which can grow to almost a metre long and live up to 120 years; these two adults were probably born long before my parents. Hovering just off the wall is a tight school of about three hundred Puget Sound rockfish. The juxtaposition of the two species exemplifies the diversity of life histories and body sizes among species of *Sebastes*, the genus to which rockfish belong. In contrast to the large and centenarian yelloweye, Puget Sound rockfish grow to only eighteen centimetres and live a mere two decades.

And the abundance goes on and on. Hundreds of black rockfish and a handful of dusky rockfish school over the anemone-covered rock ramps. Other rockfish species fill the spaces between boulders: copper, tiger, China, quillback. I am thrilled to see so many individuals near the maximum body size of their species. We ascend. Nerves are on edge as we ride the current through the kelp forest, manoeuvring to avoid tangling ourselves, re-entering the clouds of black and yellowtail rockfish.

Throughout the dive, *Festival in Bahia*, performed by McCoy Tyner and The Latin All Stars, loops as my internal soundtrack. The exuberance emitted by these jazz virtuosos mirrors the pulsing and vibrating life around us. Predatory fish are alive and well here. A glimmer into how the world used to be. A glimmer into what the world could be restored to.

No nihilism today.

OF COURSE I COULD not keep myself away from the pinnacles of Haida Gwaii. Rowan and I returned in 2010 to survey more of these current-swept hotspots, where I revelled in the kelp forests that clung to their tops. That trip I also spent lots of time on shallower, more protected reefs, helping Lynn Lee, another Ph.D. candidate in Anne's lab, with her research on invertebrate ecology. And it was through the juxtaposition of these projects that I began to see Haida Gwaii as a paradox, a patchwork of both vibrant and diminished ecosystems.

The sorts of reefs that Lynn studies often resemble a surreal version of industrial agriculture in which red urchins—voracious herbivores that mow down kelp—have primacy over most other life forms. Had Dante been diving with us, infinite fields of those spiny grazers would have infiltrated his version of hell.

To be fair, kelp-less reefs do house other life forms, including sea stars, northern abalone, sea slugs, sculpins and some rockfish. Yet these habitats are the dregs from a time before urchin numbers had run amok. Whenever our transects crossed remnant patches of kelp forest, life would light up with huge schools of juvenile rockfish hovering in the canopy, penpoint gunnels wrapping their eel-like bodies around kelp stipes, many species of crabs and snails clinging to the kelp blades, and much more. As our surveys progressed, I began to understand that the kelp forests of modern Haida Gwaii have been relegated to where strong currents or wave action keep sea urchins from carpeting the rocks.

The urchin barrens are a legacy of libertarian economics, colonial style, perpetuated by a conservation conundrum, twenty-first-century style. Between the late 1700s and early 1900s, fur traders throughout the Northeast Pacific targeted sea otters, major predators of urchins, for their valuable pelts. The traders enlisted Haida and other First Nation hunters, contributing to the erosion of "slow and small" in the relationship between indigenous cultures and the sea. The commercial hunt took about fifty thousand sea otters and drove the species to extinction in British Columbia by 1929.

Before the fur trade, sea otters kept a check on urchin numbers and behaviour, curtailing the overall impact of these spiky herbivores. During those times of vibrant tension, urchins would flee from the remains of otter-killed urchins, creating a mosaic of kelp forests and urchin patches where sea otters fed only occasionally. In the aftermath of overexploitation, such dynamics were no more. Kelp forests shrunk to a mere shadow of their old selves, taking with them the biological structures that support multitudes of fish and invertebrate species.

Twyla Bella, it seems pretty grim, doesn't it? But as we learned from *The King's Stilts*, ecosystems can roll with the punches and rebound, as long as humans give them a chance.

Extirpation of the sea otter forced an end to the trade. New laws prohibited future commercial hunts. During the 1960s and '70s, a total of eighty-nine individuals were transplanted from remnant populations in Alaska to the West Coast of Vancouver Island. From this source, British Columbia's sea otter population has grown to about five thousand and reoccupied about a third of its former range; their numbers continue to grow and spread. And wherever sea otters have reclaimed their old stomping grounds, kelp forests have begun to recover.

Yet in the southeast coast of Haida Gwaii during 2010, where I found myself estimating the diameter of yet another red urchin for the trillionth time, sea otters were nowhere to be seen. In the recent past some individuals had straggled in from far away, but their presence had been ephemeral The archipelago's isolation has, so far, precluded natural recolonization by sea otters. And a planned reintroduction by the Haida Nation and Parks Canada, who co-manage Gwaii Haanas National Park Reserve and Haida Heritage Site, is not about to happen.

This is where the conservation conundrum, twenty-first-century style, comes in. Sea otters don't just eat sea urchins— they also consume many kinds of invertebrates and some slower-moving fish, so fishers of crabs, geoducks and other commercial species view them as competitors. The apparent conflict is particularly touchy when it comes to northern abalone, which was fished into oblivion throughout British Columbia during the 1970s and '80s. Yet abalone numbers may be starting to recover in Haida Gwaii, and resuscitating a food fishery would bring tremendous social and cultural benefits to the Haida Nation. Would a sea otter reintroduction trump those benefits?

Lynn Lee has taken on that question. Beyond Haida Gwaii, her research encompasses parts of British Columbia where sea otters have re-established themselves in large or intermediate numbers. By studying kelp and abalone populations in different areas, she is examining how sea otters—perhaps managed through a subsistence hunt by the Haida and other First Nations—might allow kelp forests *and* northern abalone to recover. The structure of rocky bottoms, Lynn's data suggests, might influence the recovery potential of abalone at a local level. Complex rocky bottoms, such as boulder fields, provide hiding places; the more hiding places, the better the chances that abalone might thrive in the presence of sea otters.

And kelp forests themselves are tremendous biowealth. Beyond providing nursery habitat for rockfish of commercial value, their huge capacity to store carbon in plant tissues and slow down the rate of climate change is worth cash in carbon-trading markets. So the return of sea otters to Haida Gwaii may not be a conservation and socio-economic conundrum at all.

I see Lynn's research as a fascinating melting pot of vibrant tension, human complexity and ecosystem resilience. Her work is still unfolding. I cannot wait for her to finish composing that tale.

TWYLA BELLA, WHEN YOU were seven, in the summer of 2011, you came to Haida Gwaii and joined our research community aboard the *Victoria Rose*. Owned by Lynn, Leandre and their nine-year-old son Taimen, *Rosie* is a thirty-nine-foot ex-troller converted into a live-aboard vessel for marine research.

On Day 1 of that journey into Gwaii Haanas, you wasted no time in making a cozy home on one of *Rosie's* upper bunks, laying out your clothes, iPod and books with meticulous order along the window ledge beside your sleeping space. From then on, life on the archipelago became a mix of magic and routine, my time split between research dives and hanging out with you and Taimen on gravelly beaches and forested islands: swimming and floating on log rafts in warm weather, sheltering under tarps in the drizzle, roasting seaweed over smoky fires, exploring tide pools, helping Lynn glue tiny tags onto abalone for underwater identification, fishing from the skiff...

It was during those hangouts that I began to really see the terrestrial paradox of modern Haida Gwaii. Always looking for huckleberries, we found healthy bushes bearing fruit only rarely. The forest understory was an open moss carpet with clusters of bonsai-shaped spruces: pretty and inviting like a manicured lawn yet out of place on these islands, particularly where thistles and other exotic plants had taken hold. And the absence of cedar re-generation was very loud.

The Windy Bay blockade saved the ancient trees of Gwaii Haanas from industrial chainsaws, yet failed to repel the vacuum wrought by a lack of vibrant tension. Forest dynamics have long gone listless, "bambified" into submission by a plethora of deer. In 1878 the British Columbia Game Commission began to introduce Sitka black-tailed deer to Haida Gwaii for hunting. This was a guaranteed disaster. By the time the introductions ceased in 1925, the land was in a state of unstoppable shock.

Haida Gwaii has few natural predators to keep the intro-duced deer in check. Wolves, grizzly bears and cougars are not na-tive to the islands, and black bears make most of their living on the seashore eating salmon and intertidal invertebrates. And the forest plants of Haida Gwaii, which evolved without browsing pressure from deer, have yet to develop sufficient chemical defences to make themselves less palatable and digestible to herbivores. Under these conditions, deer became an urchin supernova gone terrestrial. Their overabundance became so extreme that even high hunt-ing rates—hunters killed more than 34,000 deer between 1976 and 1996 alone—have not kept them from overrunning the land-scape. The imbalance has spread cracks throughout the ecologi-cal foundation of the islands, eliminating songbirds that depend on understory vegetation and altering the species composition of insect communities.

Deer were not the only exotic mammals we encountered. We often saw brown rats scurrying through the intertidal rocks; this exotic species jumped ship onto the islands long ago, feeding on the young of seabirds and other species unprepared, evolutionarily, to cope with this voracious predator.

My temptation to fall back into nihilism surged here and there. But I suppressed it. I figured that this was my chance to fully accept that a world unaltered by industrialized humans was long gone, and that subsistence cultures can adapt—up to a point—to artificial shifts in resources. Our meals included venison from deer that Leandre hunted in the winter near their home on the northern part of Haida Gwaii. Access to local meat was an upside of deer overabundance and hunters, including the many locals who bag their allowable fifteen deer each year, likely play a small role in slowing down the scourge of these herbivores. But not enough and certainly not everywhere; hunters usually stay near roads or other easily accessible areas, leaving most of the archipelago risk-free for deer.

One day, while watching you and Taimen ride a log raft, I thought to myself: if this is the Anthropocene—the new geologic epoch in which humans run every show on Earth—then things are only so bad. At least so far. Here we are on what is still a gorgeous archipelago with a long and proud history of Haida culture. Unplugged. Running around on what is still a forest, splashing in what is still an ocean. And, as the recoveries of Patrol Cats and sea otters embody, ecosystems can recover from perturbations, so long as humans smarten up in time to give them a chance.

SHORTLY AFTER YOUR FIRST trip to Haida Gwaii, you began to drop by my office to help design graphs for my public presentations. When you attended one of my talks on rockfish ecology and asked questions ahead of everyone, I was beyond thrilled. The fun got even better when I needed to set up field experiments, and you jumped right into helping with the prep work. Here is that story.

The rocky reefs of Howe Sound, the fjord where we live near Vancouver, had become my local study area. On many reefs I could see an abundance of rockfish and lingcod but, unlike on the Haida Gwaii pinnacles, most of the fish here were small. I was not surprised. Howe Sound has been overfished for decades, and fisheries target the biggest individuals, ultimately reducing maximum body size within each species of predatory fish.

Our dive surveys and earlier studies told a story of ecosystem change. In the Howe Sound of today lingcod—the top predatory fish on rocky reefs—rarely exceed body lengths of eighty centimetres. But up to thirty years ago, when overfishing was just beginning, lingcod ninety to a hundred centimetres long were common.

As predators shrink, the vibrant tension of predation risk slips away. This process has a lot to do with mouth size. Predatory fish swallow prey whole, usually head or tail first, so it is impossible for them to eat prey bigger than the width and height of their open jaws. And bigger fish have bigger jaws, which makes them capable not only of consuming larger prey, but also of scaring bigger prey into adopting antipredator behaviours, such as hiding in rocky crevices. As predators shrink, big prey enter what ecologists call a size refuge; that is, big prey become invulnerable to their former predators and only small prey remain at risk.

Variants of this phenomenon—in which smaller predators become the new top predators of over-exploited communities—keep sprouting everywhere on land and in the water. Mulling over this state of affairs, it dawned on me one day that understanding how antipredator behaviour varies between different species of mesopredators while top predators are still around might help ecologists predict some impacts of fisheries. This idea emerged not from careful thought but rather from the dregs of failure.

I was running preliminary trials for a field experiment, presenting rockfish with a food reward—live shrimp of the genus *Pandalus*, tethered to chains—to later test how the presence of a large lingcod, in the form of a fibreglass model, might affect their behaviour. My expectation was that rockfish would feed on shrimp without the model lingcod—which was still being made, meticulously and *sloooowly*, by a taxidermist—but once in place the model lingcod would scare rockfish away from shrimp: a slam dunk into experimental evidence showing that large lingcod affect the feeding rates of rockfish on invertebrate prey. Patrol Cats to

Nizzards kind of stuff. Not quite the link from Patrol Cats to the survival of the entire Kingdom of Binn, but certainly an important first step towards figuring out the rocky reef version of that story. Simple. And, as it turned out, horribly rockfish-centric.

A different mesopredator was quick to remind me that reality can derail well-dreamt experiments. During the preliminary trials, kelp greenling—which I had barely thought about so far—kept nailing shrimp ahead of everyone else. Rockfish were abundant on the reefs and did attack shrimp, but at a much slower rate than kelp greenling. And it was not a mere matter of kelp greenling being quicker at finding shrimp; video from fixed video cameras showed that rockfish were often first to inspect shrimp from a distance. Perhaps rockfish were being more suspicious than kelp greenling about the chains and plastic ties that tethered the shrimp. After all, these were novel structures that reef fish had not evolved with, so species differences in willingness to attack shrimp could turn out to be interesting.

Still, I was not enjoying what appeared to be a waste of my funds and get-wet-and-cold currency. I would go home after a field day, hang my dripping dry suit from the porch rafters, crank up some angry rock music and review video footage from fixed cameras while trying to summon loving thoughts about kelp greenling. Eventually, those thoughts crystallized into two words: life history.

Thanks to kelp greenling, I realized that the reef mesopredators of Howe Sound—including juvenile lingcod at risk of cannibalism from adult lingcod—encompassed a spectrum of lifestyle speeds. Copper and quillback rockfish were at the slow end of the spectrum. Copper rockfish live to fifty years and usually do not reproduce until they are six to seven years old, while quillback rockfish live close to a century and normally do not start reproducing until age eleven to twenty. To top it all, rockfish mothers tend to produce more abundant and stronger young as they age. For such fish, producing the most offspring during their lives may require living cautiously and avoiding predators—even at the cost of missing out on meals. This is especially true for quillbacks, which live longer and begin reproducing later in life.

Lingcod and kelp greenling, on the other hand, are at the fast end of the lifestyle spectrum. They begin reproducing earlier in life than rockfish, and the oldest lingcod and kelp greenling recorded were, respectively, thirty-five and twelve years. For them, living dangerously to secure food that enhances short-term reproduction may produce the most offspring during their lives. This may be particularly true for the shorter-lived kelp greenling, the live-fast, die-young predator of Howe Sound's reefs.

So there you have it: a new hypotheses emerging from the scraps of a failed experiment. And a testable one to boot. All four mesopredators eat the same kinds of shrimp and all are eaten by a common enemy: adult lingcod, the lion of the temperate reef.

The fibreglass lingcod model arrived in late October. Cast from a female lingcod caught in Alaska, it was over a metre long, and fierce and beautiful. There was no time to dawdle. From our long-term studies we knew that in about five weeks rockfish would begin to increase the time they spent holed up inside crevices. We needed to complete our experiments before that seasonal shift could bias results, but with the potential for November storms around the corner, the odds of doing so were slim.

Yet we had to try and, as it turned out, we were lucky. Field day after field day the seas were calm, the water clear, the air near-freezing under crisp blue skies. Working with colleagues from the Vancouver Aquarium, Donna Gibbs and Jeff Marliave, I spent many dives tethering live shrimp to chains, setting up the model lingcod and the video cameras that would record the action, getting the hell out for three to four hours, and returning to retrieve our junk and survey the fish and the invertebrates.

Every time I tightened a monofilament loop to tether a shrimp, I smiled thinking back on the previous night when you, Twyla Bella, had pre-tied the loops. To borrow the term you invented when you were five: the experiments were "hundreds of work." And a blast.

The results were way cool. Kelp greenling, which live the fastest lifestyle, took the highest risks and were the only species to attack shrimp close to the model lingcod. Subadult lingcod only attacked shrimp when these were far from the lingcod, and copper rockfish attacked shrimp only when the lingcod was entirely absent from the reef. Quillback rockfish, which live the slowest lifestyle, took the least risks, never leaving the areas near their rocky shelters to attack the shrimp.

The lesson from all this is that different species of reef mesopredators, despite occupying similar positions in the food web, do not necessarily play the same ecological role. Some respond more strongly to predation risk than others, and we can predict these differences from their life history characteristics. This sort of insight can help ecologists predict how ecosystems might change if people continue to eliminate top predators.

The study also made me realize that we should keep a closer eye on kelp greenling. With their greater gusto for risk-taking and lower appeal to fishers—who would rather eat lingcod and rockfish—this species could well be rising to become the new top dog of overfished reefs. We have already seen this scenario in action on land, where former top predators like wolves have been replaced by mesopredators with faster life histories like coyotes.

TWYLA BELLA, THE OVEREXPLOITATION of top predators, the impact of exotic deer, and the rise of smaller predators up the food chain are already serious enough problems. But my thoughts cannot stop there. I now spend a lot of my time thinking about how our carbon dioxide emissions indirectly alter predator-prey interactions.

The oceans absorb one-third of all the extra carbon dioxide we dump into the atmosphere and are becoming acidified. This change in chemistry alters the physiology of many species, deactivating the antipredator responses of some prey and diminishing the hunting abilities of some predators. Many prey, for instance, hide in response to the scent emitted by individuals just killed or injured by predators. As ocean acidification intensifies, some species of fish larvae are likely to hide less and succumb to predators more often. The other side of the coin is that acidification lowers the metabolism and movements of large predators like jumbo squid, which might allow prey to hide less and feed more, indirectly impacting lower parts of the food web. As you can see, figuring out the net impact of ocean acidification on vibrant tension is a daunting, unresolved challenge.

You can say the same for ocean warming. As sea temperatures rise, top predators that tolerate warmer water or prefer ice-free conditions—like great white sharks moving north to Alaska or killer whales expanding into the melting Arctic—enter new areas where prey are unprepared for that novel surge of predation risk. The other side of that coin is that top predators that like it cool—including salmon sharks, blue sharks and mako sharks—are becoming increasingly confined to shrinking pockets of cold water and losing access to prey that are physiologically capable of staying put in the warming water.

Beyond changing species distributions, ocean warming also lowers the oxygen content of the water. These stressful conditions hamper the capacity of fish to grow, and appear to be on their way to shrinking the body sizes of entire fish communities. The effects might resemble those of overfishing: shrunken fish have smaller mouths and therefore impose predation risk only on smaller prey, turning food webs topsy-turvy.

How do warmer water, lower oxygen, acidification and over-fishing *combine* to reshape predator-prey interactions? As you can see, ecologists are not about to run out of things to ponder. Neither are parents of young children.

To cope with these thoughts, I send my mind back to a day near the end of your first trip to Haida Gwaii. That day all adults were needed for the tasks at hand and we dropped you and Taimen on the beach. Knowing there were no grizzly bears or cougars on the archipelago, it seemed safe enough to leave a seven-year-old and a nine-year-old alone on a remote island. Okay, that sounds over-dramatic, particularly because you had a radio and I could see you from half a kilometre away while I tended divers from the skiff. Still, that was a big leap into the next stage of your development and my experience as a parent.

Perhaps it was then, Twyla Bella, that I began to understand that I cannot, in any possible way (except a delusional one), be responsible for handing down an entire world to you. Only society as a whole, through democratic institutions and with each of us as essential players, can make or break the future. My responsibility is to hand down to you the stories and tools that will allow you to deal with a rapidly changing world and do what you can to steer that new world towards a path of greater resilience.

It began to rain hard. I watched you and Taimen through binoculars as you gathered your packs and clambered over slimy boulders on the beach, eventually finding shelter underneath an overhanging cliff. A trivial thing for anybody else to witness, but your resourcefulness reassured and warmed my heart, endlessly.

Love,
Pops

CHAPTER 4

Climate and War

Dear Twyla Bella,

I first saw W. Eugene Smith's photo *A Walk To Paradise Garden* when I was thirteen. In this black-and-white image from 1946, the photographer's young children walk, hand in hand, from darkness into the light at the edge of a forest canopy. The moment I saw it I was drawn into a world of contrasts that emanated as much from the luminosity of that forest edge as from the horror of Smith's earlier work.

In 1944 and 1945, on the Pacific islands of Iwo Jima, Saipan and Okinawa, Smith had followed American soldiers as they battled the Japanese. Snapping photos as they died. Snapping photos as they killed. Snapping photos as one soldier stared wearily from under the canopy of his helmet at a wounded, naked baby dying in his hands, while a second soldier—cigarette in mouth, legs spread forward in a stable stance, hip-high rifle at the ready—looked past the dying infant and straight into, I imagine, the photographer's soul. Committed to bringing back the war to whoever was willing to see it for what it really was, Smith was taking a picture in Okinawa on May 23, 1945, when a Japanese shell fragment went right through the hand that held the camera, blasting into his head and face. Survival surgeries. Pain. No photography. Until, more than a year later, he captured the antithesis of Okinawa, *A Walk To Paradise Garden*.

To my teenage self, Smith's images encapsulated the breadth of humanity. Whatever that soldier staring towards Smith had seen, I, too, wanted to see. Whatever those children were walking into, I, too, wanted to enter.

So I fantasized about becoming a war photographer. Yet, whether it was legitimate contingencies or the reality that I was plain chicken, I became an ecologist. Like many of my colleagues, I entered the discipline because I loved wild places and wanted to make my living by spending time in them. I wanted to study mountain sheep (which I did), marine predators (which I do) and ancient rainforests (which I helped others do). But as time goes by, the line between Smith's work and that of some environmental scientists keeps blurring in ways not entirely metaphorical.

In February 2012, I found myself in a seminar room, attending a meeting of the American Association for the Advancement of Science. The session, organized by the Asia-Pacific Center for Security Studies, a U.S. Department of Defense academic institute, focused on climate change impacts on Bangladesh. The statistics were staggering. Some 80 percent of the country is twelve metres above sea level or less. Not surprisingly, a fifth of Bangladesh floods in an average year and nearly 70 percent of the country has flooded in extreme years. As climate change continues to melt the ice caps, sea levels rise higher. Flooding not only wrecks infrastructure and drowns people but also hampers agricultural production by increasing soil salinity. The 1970 Bhola cyclone produced a storm surge that killed half a million people in the low-lying Ganges delta that encompasses present-day Bangladesh. The cyclone was an extreme event but—according to time series analyses by NASA climatologist James Hansen and colleagues— extreme weather anomalies occurred ten times more frequently between 1980 and 2010 than during the preceding thirty years. These changes can be attributed to human-caused climate change, which implies that Bhola-type catastrophes could become a new normal in the foreseeable future.

And there is more. Bangladesh has fifty-four rivers that originate upstream in India. As climate change reduces the mass of the Himalayan glaciers that feed these rivers, water scarcity will threaten agriculture in both countries. Yet India, which already is building a security fence along its border with Bangladesh, clearly has the upper hand. As rivers dry and agricultural production crashes, India could decide to hoard that water and keep desperate Bangladeshi migrants outside their fence. When you consider the population density of Bangladesh—over a thousand people per square kilometre, most in abject poverty—it is easy to imagine how diminished Himalayan glaciers and rising sea levels might promote regional chaos. Similar tensions could arise from the drying of rivers shared between India and Pakistan, two nations that have nuclear weapons and a history of antagonism. No wonder the U.S. military is interested in climate change.

The challenges of the Indian subcontinent are not unique. It is not a big stretch to predict that resource scarcity, which is directly linked to climate, will cause more frequent armed conflicts around the globe. To understand why, allow me to digress into the world of evolutionary theory and behavioural ecology. When we return to war in a few pages, it will be with new insights.

DURING THE 1980s, ECOLOGISTS began to develop mathematical models of animal behaviour that are state-dependent. That is, these models examine how an animal's current "state"—its age, body condition and other factors—affects its behavioural responses to the trade-off between antipredator and feeding behaviours. (Recall from my earlier stories that antipredator behaviours may keep prey from getting eaten, but also limit where, when and how much prey can eat.) These models predict that declining resources should increase an animal's risk-taking as well as predation rates for prey attempting to avoid starvation or losing reproductive potential.

To get a sense of what I mean, imagine a young animal in good shape with access to ample resources. This animal has the potential for many more reproductive bouts, and therefore aims for lots of safety while feeding just enough to maintain good body condition. Now imagine an older animal during a drought.

Skinny and worn out, it might get another chance at reproduction, perhaps its last, but only if it feeds enough to improve its body condition. Between a rock and hard place, with few reproductive assets worth protecting into the future, it may as well risk greater exposure to predators to find better food. If it gets killed, at least it tried. Beats hiding and starving. It also beats staying alive without reproducing, which—unless the animal is young enough to expect future chances to make up for lost reproductive time—is the same as being dead, in evolutionary terms. (Eusocial species—which include wolves, naked mole rats, ants, bees and termites—are an exception. In these species, groups of relatives reproduce cooperatively. Only some individuals—such as the alpha pair of a wolf pack or the queen of a beehive—reproduce directly, while others perpetuate a portion of their genes by helping their reproductive relatives raise young or acquire resources.)

Real-world data agree with these ideas. In the 1990s, ecologists conducted experiments in which they exposed bullfrog tadpoles to predation risk from larval dragonflies under contrasting levels of food abundance. Tadpoles experiencing low food levels moved one and half times more often and at higher speeds than tadpoles experiencing high food levels. Higher movement rates under food scarcity, which reflect greater foraging effort, also increased exposure to predators and caused a near doubling of predation rates, even though the number of predators remained constant. These and later experiments suggest that synergisms between resources and predators are fundamental to population and community processes, and that prey behaviour is inherent to these synergisms. These processes scale up to vast landscapes. Wildebeests in poor body condition, for instance, spend more time in habitats with better food but higher predation risk, and thus get killed more often by lions than do wildebeests in better condition that use safer habitats with less food.

Seeking to generalize these ideas to other ecosystems, in 2000 I travelled to Shark Bay, a large marine park spanning seven and half thousand square kilometres in Western Australia, where I spent much of my time jumping off skiffs to capture and tag green turtles. I was working with Mike Heithaus, now a professor at Florida International University; at the time we both were Ph.D. candidates at Simon Fraser University in Vancouver, working under the supervision of Larry Dill, a giant of behavioural ecology and a hugely influential mentor to us both.

Mike had already been studying tiger sharks for three years and had started the turtle project. He had been attracted to Shark Bay in part because the density of tiger sharks—the top predators—changes seasonally, predictably from year to year. The sharks are most abundant during the warm summer months but their numbers drop to very low levels during winter. The end result is a huge natural experiment in which the level of predation risk varies in time across an entire ecosystem. A dream come true for ecologists like us, eager to test big ideas in big places outside the artificial confines of a lab.

From Mike's earlier work we knew that tiger sharks tend to hang out around seagrass banks, where the water is only two metres deep or less and food for the sharks' prey—green turtles, bottlenose dolphins, dugongs, and pied cormorants —is most abundant. (Green turtles and dugongs feed on the seagrasses while bottlenose dolphins and pied cormorants eat fish that live on seagrass habitats.) Deeper channels with sandy bottoms surround the seagrass banks; these have few sharks but little food, so green turtles and other species eaten by sharks face a trade-off between finding food and risking death at the seagrass banks.

During our study, I noticed great variation in the body condition of individual green turtles. This was very exciting to us, as Mike and I recognized this opportunity to test predictions derived from models of state-dependent behaviour. Over the course of our study, which eventually spanned seven years of data, we discovered that turtles in poor body condition venture far into the interior areas of seagrass banks, where the nutritional quality of the seagrasses is superior to that at the edge of the habitat. This finding excited us even more because interior areas are also more dangerous. Here turtles encountering a tiger shark can escape only in two dimensions, horizontally, and cannot bolt into deep water.

In contrast, turtles in good body condition prefer the edges of sea-grass banks, where food is not as good but danger is lower because they have three dimensions for escape: horizontally and down into the deep adjacent channels.

Seasonal variation highlighted how body condition, food and predator presence combine to affect risk-taking decisions. Turtles in really good condition ventured towards the interior of seagrass banks only during winter, when shark densities were at a predictable annual low, while turtles in the worst body condition always used the interior of seagrass banks. Even during the season of low shark abundance, turtles in good body condition stayed closer to the bank edge than their skinnier counterparts. Because food quality is lower at the edge than at the interior of banks, these observations match predictions from models of state-dependent behaviour. When I look at the graphs of that study, it is almost as if beautiful modeling equations had danced off the page and onto the seagrass banks.

The theory of state-dependent behaviour can have profound implications for ecological conservation because humans influence the global distribution and abundance of resources used by all living things. Models I have developed, for example, predict that overfishing can force harbour seals and Steller's sea lions in western Alaska to increase the frequency of their deep foraging dives at the cost of increased exposure to Pacific sleeper sharks, which feed in deep water. In addition, deep dives are longer than shallower ones and demand a longer period of oxygen recovery at the surface, which could increase exposure to shallow-water predators like killer whales. Through these changes in feeding behaviour, overfishing may indirectly increase predation rates on both harbour seals and Steller's sea lions, potentially contributing to declining trends for some populations.

Another prediction is that climate change, which affects resource availability, can indirectly alter animals' rates of mortality. This prediction might help us anticipate and perhaps mitigate conflicts between humans and certain large carnivores, such as polar bears. Under normal sea ice conditions, polar bears are successful hunters of seals, which they target when the seals surface at breathing holes on the ice pack. When the ice is good, bears remain fat and healthy, so they have no need to approach human settlements. Yet the option for polar bears to avoid humans is diminishing as climate change reduces the permanence of the ice pack. In western Hudson Bay, the sea ice is breaking up earlier in the spring, which has lengthened the period when polar bears are unable to hunt seals and have to fast on land. As a result, more hungry polar bears in search of human-related foods are showing up at settlements, and people are having to kill more bears in self-protection.

No matter what scale of the animal world we choose to look at—from tadpoles at risk from dragonfly larvae (or even smaller predators and prey) to wildebeest at risk from lions and polar bears at risk from humans—prey organisms play it cool and safe whenever their food is easily accessible and their body condition is good. Taking away some of that food limits the choice to avoid risk. Taking away most of it seriously ups the stakes, virtually eliminating the choice to play it safe.

WHICH BRINGS US BACK to war. Why does it pervade human history? Clearly, there is no single answer to that question. But one thing the paleoclimatic and historical records do suggest is that humans are not exempt from our own form of state-dependent behaviour. Historically, climate-driven resource shortages have influenced the decision by hungry societies to initiate wars that might never have happened had people been well fed. A team of geographers pieced together evidence suggesting that during the Little Ice Age, which occurred between the fifteenth and nineteenth centuries, dips in global temperatures coincided with increases in the numbers of wars worldwide. Consistent with theory on state-dependent behaviour, drops in agricultural production and rising food prices appear to have been the factors mediating climatic stress and war.

And the Little Ice Age is not an isolated fluke. Think of El Niño Southern Oscillation (ENSO)—an oceanographic cycle that influences global climate, alternating between warmer and drier El Niño phases and moister and cooler La Niña phases. Data spanning from 1950 to 2004 shows that, in ninety-three tropical countries strongly affected by ENSO, armed conflicts were twice as likely to arise during starker El Niño phases than they were during more lush La Niña ones. In contrast, in eighty-two temperate countries where ENSO effects are weak, effectively serving as controls in a natural experiment, the timing of armed conflicts was unrelated to ENSO

Although ENSO and the Little Ice Age do not necessarily provide a road map for future effects of human-caused climate change, they do suggest that the general relationship between climatic stress and war—with resource and economic scarcity as likely mediating factors—is real. In addition, volatility appears to have risen in dry regions of Africa and other resource-stressed parts of the world, as the frequencies of drought or other unfavourable conditions increase under climate change. In all of these cases it would be wrong to call climate change the *direct* cause of conflict. But there is good reason to think of climate change and resource scarcity as strong winds that fan the flames of state-depending behaviour, increasing the willingness by people to engage in violence. According to Chris Huhne, the British secretary of state for energy and climate change between 2010 and 2012, "Climate change is a threat multiplier. It will make unstable states more unstable and conflict more likely."

Humans. We who change the Earth's climate. We who, against evolutionary odds, extend compassion beyond our kin. We who create global instititutions such as the United Nations, which, for all their faults, were born from a desire to promote peace. We who are capable of marvellous intelligence and unbelievable stupidity. For us, the past need not be a mirror for the future. But it sure is an ominous warning.

TWYLA BELLA, DURING THE early 1990s, your mother and I were in our twenties. It was an era of freedom, adventure and intellectual exploration. We had come to Kluane National Park in the Yukon to conduct field research for my master's thesis and to experience a living, breathing landscape with its full component of large carnivores.

My memories of those March mornings are vivid. A snow-pack of granular crystals covered the frozen Slims River, the surrounding mountains and the icy vastness of Kluane Lake. Only the south-facing slopes of Sheep Mountain, swept by winds descending from mammoth ice fields and funnelling down the river valley, remained free of snow. There, orange bands of rock mixed with brown scree slopes to diversify winter's canvas. Like ghosts floating on a lunar landscape, Dall's sheep, northern relatives of bighorn sheep, moved across the barren slopes. Their coats white as the adjacent glaciers, they were easy to spot against the dark background of their snowless and rocky winter range. On a knoll overlooking the slopes, Gail and I would sit and watch them, our stillness interrupted only by the click-clack of computer keys, adjustments to spotting scopes and bouts of uncontrollable shivering. The temperature on those mornings regularly dipped below minus twenty Celsius, not particularly cold by local standards, but cold enough to make studying the second-by-second feeding and antipredator behaviours of Dall's sheep challenging work.

Lee Gass, an ecologist at the University of British Columbia co-supervising my research at the time, has compared this kind of data collection to a dance between two partners: the animal and the human observer. The animal acts and the researcher reacts, physically and without conscious thought, by pressing the corresponding computer keys. In this way we encoded events in the life of individual Dall's sheep—steps, vigilant postures, aggressive interactions, feeding motions—into electronic glyphs to be deciphered later.

Over time, I pieced together how Dall's sheep managed the conflicting demands of finding food and not getting killed by wolves or coyotes: forming groups of different sizes (less predation in a bigger group, but more aggressive interactions with other sheep), splitting their time between open, steep rocky terrain (where safety is greater but food patchier) and the edges of thick vegetation (where food is richer but an ambush more likely). In April we encountered our first grizzly bear of the season, just out of hibernation and adding to the list of predators that Dall's sheep had to avoid. In May, with lambs recently born, the mothers had to be extra vigilant for golden eagles that may knock their young off the cliffs and then pick up a meal at the bottom.

Our stay was meant to last only the few months planned for the study. But this was not to happen. Gail and I became enraptured by the northern landscape and its fascinating mix of people: native cultures who have lived in place for countless generations and fringe characters who have come there to reinvent themselves in an unconventional world. After defending my thesis, we settled for the long term in the southwest Yukon, alternating our time between research contracts (history for Gail, ecology for me), Gail's emerging career in modern dance, and exploring the vastness of the Yukon and the neighbouring Alaskan coast. Blasting through remote glaciers on skis. Running rivers in kayaks. Blissfully unaware that, in a parallel universe, genocides were unfolding in Rwanda and the former Yugoslavia.

Some years later, I descended from that cloud and confronted images of Rwanda's Kagera River clogged with mutilated corpses; eight hundred thousand people hacked to death with machetes in a hundred days. For a time, these images took hold of me. How could such extreme horror come to be? Resource scarcity was not the direct cause—myriad historical and socio-political factors can take credit for that. But according to two economists studying northwest Rwanda between 1988 and 1993—the five years leading to the genocide—land degradation and resource scarcity were the dry, hot winds that fanned tensions between the Tutsi, who controlled a majority of resources in rural areas, and the Hutu, who were increasingly needy for those resources. The economists—Catherine André and Jean-Philippe Platteau at the Université de Namur in Belgium—found that the "prevailing state of extreme land hunger created a troubled environment which made the most desperate people (particularly young people with only bleak prospects) ready to seize any opportunity to change their present predicament." And these conditions go "a long way towards explaining why violence spread so quickly and so devastatingly throughout the countryside."

In other words, resource scarcity pushed individuals already at the edge into an abyss where they could dehumanize their neighbours into mere "cockroaches"—as Hutu propaganda branded the Tutsi—obstructing access to land. Once inside that abyss, horrors such as that recounted by Dr. James Orbinski, head of mission for Médecins Sans Frontières during the Rwandan genocide, became routine:

> One night, after many long hours of surgery, a girl of about nine told me how she had escaped murder at the hands of the killing squads. The squads were part of an organized government plan to erase the existence of the Tutsi people from Rwanda. Through an interpreter, the girl told me, "My mother hid me in the latrines. I saw through the hole. I watched them hit her with machetes. I watched my mother's arm fall into my father's blood on the floor, and I cried without making noise in the toilet."

A DAY IN JUNE 2006 at Annie Lake, near Whitehorse, Yukon: the place known as Désdélé Méné to the Carcross/Tagish people, who call this region their ancestral home. You, Twyla Bella, are two and a half years old. The ice melt still recent. The water surface calm. Rugged mountains all around. Dall's sheep mothers and their lambs visible up high, among the crags. Common loons float on the lake. Wolf scats lie in the nearby forest. This valley, our home for eleven years. The placenta that you and Gail shared while you were in the womb lies buried at the shore of the nearby Watson River. Broken down by detritivores, its essence now drifts into the river that connects with the Southern Lakes, the Yukon River and eventually the Arctic Ocean. The physical bond with your mother has become indistinguishable from the land, the flowing waters.

Twyla Bella, fate has been good to us. Happy historical accidents have placed us in a vastly different world from that of Rwanda in 1994. But, given that we are the descendents of Jews who left Europe just before the Holocaust—with all our relatives who remained, save four survivors, dying in Nazi concentration camps—the fate of that Rwandan girl is not completely unconnected to our family history. Worse. Fates comparable to that of the Rwandan family continue to play themselves out today in many places where resource scarcity pushes people with existing grievances into dark places.

World War II, all wars past, current and future, may seem far away from this valley. Yet I also knew that warring raids among the indigenous peoples of southwestern Yukon occurred as recently as the mid-nineteenth century. Even the Inuit, arguably among the most egalitarian societies that has ever existed, have waged bloody feuds over resources.

I like to believe that humans have the capacity to take ownership of our history, both evolutionary and otherwise, and transcend it while acknowledging our origins. Sure, we are vulnerable to evolutionary drives, such as those that govern state-dependent behaviour. But we are not necessarily bound by them. My father, your *abuelo*, was born into a dysfunctional household, raised with violence and amidst mental illness. He could have slipped into dysfunction but chose not to. To me, his ability to muster that much self-awareness is a sign that people can learn to recognize our vulnerability to evolutionary drives or other historical forces while choosing not to act on them. If that awareness were to propagate, then perhaps society might treat climate change as the world emergency it is and act in ways that respect intergenerational justice.

We place the canoe on the water. Your friend Ensio, only a couple of years older, helps you into it. A glimmer, to my biased eyes, of W. Eugene Smith's *A Walk To Paradise Garden*. We glide on the canoe towards the wetland where we will collect medicinal plants: coltsfoot and *Artemisia tilesii*. Plants that strengthen our connection to the Earth.

Love,
Pops

The Genius
Who Invented Walking

I walk through the forest with seven-year-old Twyla Bella when, out of nowhere, she asks: "Who invented walking?"

I do my best to recount the story of *Australopithecus afarensis* and other hominids from the African savannahs and forests of more than three million years ago.

... how those first steps became us...

After a poignant silence, she remarks:

"Whoever invented walking was a genius."

Within my mind, I ask her future self:

"Must genius and destroyer be the same?"

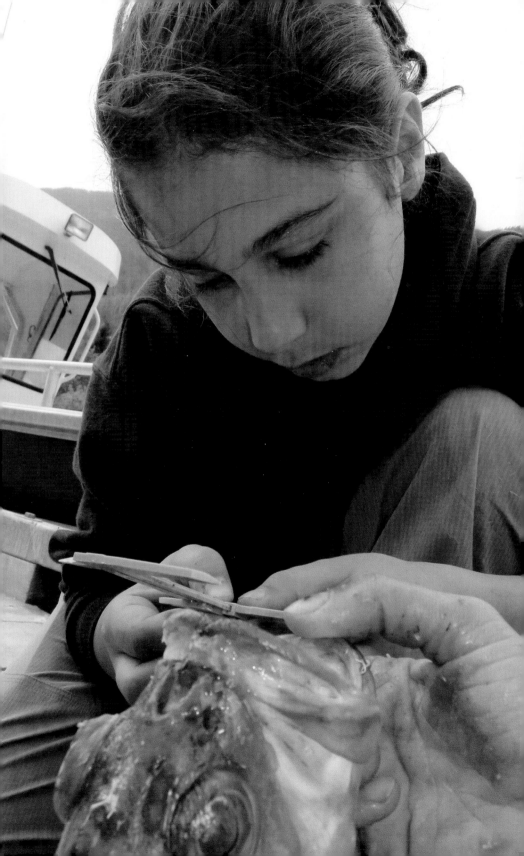

Wild Food

Dear Twyla Bella,

I want to tell you about our origins.

In the short term, we descend from Jews who barely missed the Holocaust. Perhaps for that reason, I often find myself obsessed with genocide. I have gone through periods when I devoured literature and films on this topic, trying to make sense of the horror. Why do we—the species with the greatest potential for an altruism that extends beyond immediate relatives—insist on sinking to such despicable acts against our own kind?

But in the longer term, and at a deeper level, all humans descend from hunter-gatherers. This way of life dominates our evolutionary history. Our deepest psyche. We need to be nourished by wild plants and wild animals. I, in particular, need the exchange with our non-human relatives that hunting, fishing and gathering facilitate. Without it, my world view is much diminished. I hope you continue to grow up experiencing, to the extent that our place and times can allow, that connection with our wild relatives.

So we descend from Jews who were lucky enough to evade the Holocaust *and* from hunting, fishing and gathering people. This has helped me understand a connection between the degrading of the biosphere and crimes against indigenous cultures that subsist on wild things. Having been raised in Mexico City, I did not encounter the world view of hunter-gatherers until I was a young adult. I can almost pinpoint the moment when I first began to gain entry into that cosmology.

IT WAS LATE AUGUST 1987. I was squatting by the Peel River, near the border between the Yukon and the Northwest Territories, waiting for a ride to take me to the Richardson Mountains. I was not in a hurry to get there; after two months of working with the Canadian Wildlife Service, studying birds on the Arctic tundra next to the Beaufort Sea, I was hungry for human contact. And I welcomed the rediscovered feeling of trees nearby.

I was a solo traveller. No one I had talked to—the Inuvialiut soapstone carver at the Tuktoyaktuk gravel spit, the Gwich'in kids on their bikes by the Peel River—knew where I had been. No one knew where I was going.

Hours passed. The few vehicles on the Dempster Highway were RVs that refused to stop. Eventually, I gave up and approached a man who worked on the ferry that crossed the Peel River. Jim was an Inuvialiut from Tuktoyaktuk who knew the place where I had spent the summer studying red-throated loons; he had done much hunting in the same area. I told him I was going to the Richardson Mountains. He chuckled and informed me that besides being full of grizzlies they were cold, miserable and covered with wet snow. I replied, "After two months on the tundra, I'm fairly brain damaged." Jim chuckled again, confessing that when he was younger he also had walked the tundra, "for the hell of it."

Jim took me to his summer tent, where his five-year-old daughter Charlene, his wife Esther (a Gwich'in) and Esther's father sat by the wood stove sipping tea. He brought me a smoked whitefish from the nearby smokehouse. "Bait for the griz?" I asked in joking appreciation.

After tea, Charlene and I made drawings on the ground and sang aloud. We played hide-and-seek and chased each other by the river. Perhaps it was then, Twyla Bella, that I realized that if I ever had a child of my own, I would want her to be a daughter. When it began to rain heavily, Esther told me the family was to spend the night in nearby Fort McPherson, but I was welcome to stay in their tent.

I joined Jim, who worked on the ferry until one in the morning. We sat on deck, chatting about the Far North, my early life in Mexico City, mountaineering (my passion at that time) and hunting. I told Jim that hunting was meaningless in my upbringing. I had read an essay by mountaineer Galen Rowell about a mountain goat doing "climbs" that seemed divorced from any survival value. Rowell hinted that the goat had been seeking adventure the way a mountaineer would. While I had questioned its scientific validity, I had accepted the tale as a philosophy. I liked to think that, when basic survival needs had been met, sheer mystery and adventure were reasons enough for animals and native people to explore the mountains and tundra. So there we were; the urbanite who had grown-up on supermarket food chatting away while the subsistence hunter listened politely. It all sounded so passionate. So true.

But then it was Jim's turn to speak, and his words triggered the beginning of a shift in my perspective. Jim had grown up on the Arctic coast where, not long ago, survival had depended almost completely on hunting. In those days, before the arrival of Hudson's Bay Company stores, famines used to wipe out small settlements. In this sense northern cultures truly were part of the ecosystem, having population cycles with highs and lows that depended on the availability of prey. Jim always had a tangible reason for going to the tundra and pack ice: caribou and seals. Famines are now gone from the Arctic, but hunting remained a practical necessity amidst unemployment and the high cost of foods imported from the south. But to express the significance of hunting in such simplistic economic terms trivialized the real point. The hunt, Jim said, is identity; it defines culture and the relationship between the people and the land. Natives believe in conservation because they want an abundance of animals to hunt; it would be wrong, even dangerous, to disrespect their non-human relatives.

As Jim talked, I began to see mountaineering as the product of industrialized society and not something that subsistence hunters or mountain goats would naturally pursue. "I always hunt in the easiest way," Jim claimed. He always used a snowmobile and you would never catch him on snowshoes. No wonder Charlene asked about hitchhikers, "Where are their trucks? Isn't it silly to walk to town?" About canoeists, she asked, "Where are their motorboats?" Jim always gave the same answer: "They are just into self-imposed punishment." Through these apparently disparaging statements, I understood that Jim was inviting me to see the obvious: isolation and a severe winter that lasts most of the year do not make living or hunting easy, no matter what tools you use.

Eventually, Jim left to join his family in Fort McPherson. I spent the night among howling dogs and rambunctious ravens. After waking by the river in the still dawn, I ate breakfast on the tent's doorstep, among fat ravens that strutted like campaigning politicians.

Two Gwich'in, John and Johnny, gave me a ride in their muddy semi. They drove me to the mountains, telling tales of hunting moose and watching a plane crash. Eventually, they dropped me off where the Dempster Highway entered a gorge that penetrated the Richardson Mountains. Donning my backpack, heading into the cool tundra air, I felt like a kid finishing the last day of school. The leaves of dwarf birch, willow and blueberry had ignited with the reds and yellows of autumn. Tree sparrows sang in the willows and a pair of common snipes flushed from the tussocks. The birdlife of these mountains is unusual. During the Pleistocene glaciation that ended twelve thousand years ago, much of the Arctic coast and adjacent areas were covered with ice, but the Richardson Mountains remained ice-free, attracting seabirds and shorebirds from the coastal tundra. Nesting long-tailed jaegers and surfbirds brought a certain mystique to this alpine terrain.

Under breaking skies I wandered up and down ridges, creeks and valleys. The silence was so complete that I could almost hear the sun's rays spreading patches of brightness. In the valley bottom a female northern harrier hovered above the willows, dived and then rose with a ground squirrel in her talons. The load must have been too heavy, for she dropped down and tried to rise twice more.

On her fourth attempt she let go of the squirrel and then dived into the willows after it, perhaps to feast on the ground.

It rained through the night and in the morning I walked in a world diffused by thin mist and subdued sunlight. I travelled slowly, pausing to eat rain-covered fruits of bearberry, cranberry and blueberry. Drenched by fog and rain, I ascended to a pass and dropped into the next valley until the weather forced me to set up camp.

Two days later, I climbed to a high pass and watched the fog dissipate. I saw light shift shadows over gullies, rounded hills, sharp ridges. Descending into the next valley, I followed brooks, not really caring if my view of native and animal attitudes towards adventure was right or wrong; even if my journey was the product of an affluent and industrialized society, this moment was real enough.

Still. Jim's words echoed within me, raising questions about hollow spots within my world view.

The next morning my tent collapsed under blasting wind and rain. I decided that enough was enough and embarked on a five-hour, high-speed marathon to the Dempster Highway. If Jim could have seen me then, he would have had a good laugh. The sight of a golden eagle overhead energized me and I charged through the wet, tussocky tundra. But soon I became bogged down in tall willows and imagined hidden grizzlies, sent by Jim, waiting to devour me.

Eventually I reached the highway—civilization, warmth, food! Not yet, for the Dempster was silent. In the heavy rain I hopped like a madman, but the attempt to maintain my body heat was futile. To distract myself from the uncontrollable shivering I composed a self-obituary that featured the words "hypothermia" and "nobody knew where he was going." But a divine apparition suddenly told me to not get ahead of myself. It was John, the same Gwich'in man who had driven me to the mountains some days before, sticking his head out the window of his muddy semi, grinning broadly. As rain turned to snow, he drove us towards cookies and coffee; my mind trying to grasp this merging of the modern and the traditional, the trucker and the hunter, all in one.

MUCH LATER, IN 2002—after years of experiencing hunting and gathering through direct practice and research related to wildlife use by indigenous people and other hunters—I found myself in our Yukon home, flipping through *The Economist*, when this headline stopped me in my tracks: "No more hunting and gathering." The article read:

> "Where I lived before, I killed animals and ate the meat. When the rain fell I got wild fruits. But I didn't have enough water. The government asked me to move here." Nyatsang Dira, a man in his 70s, stands under the glaring sun in dusty New Xade, a newly-created village on the edge of Botswana's Kalahari desert. He is one of some 2,000 Basarwa, or San Bushmen, evicted by the government from the parched Central Kalahari Game Reserve since 1997. Just a few dozen, mostly old men, remain in the reserve. One of Africa's last nomadic cultures is about to be snuffed out.
>
> Botswana's president, Festus Mogae, says that "hunting and gathering is no longer a viable way of life." In New Xade the government provides a school, a hostel for children whose parents work on farms far away, financial compensation, boreholes for water, a new road, cattle, sheep and welfare payments. It is the sort of official attention that few Africans enjoy.
>
> But a walk around the settlement shows that many Basarwa find modern life difficult. Alcoholism seems rife; one of the village's four policemen says assaults and drunkenness are common. To deter rising crime, goat thieves are now jailed for five years. And the worst thing about New Xade? Said one villager, there are no wild fruits.

Twyla Bella, I have chosen to stick to our bioregion, so it is unlikely that I will ever go to the Kalahari. Yet an inkling of what "No more hunting and gathering" might mean to the San came to me a few years later, after we moved to southern British Columbia, while walking through the forest with my friend Bob Semeniuk. Bob has seen a lot of the best and the worst of humanity while covering wars and the plight of traditional peoples in many parts of the world, including prostitution and AIDS amidst the relocated San. As we walked through the forests near our home in search of oyster mushrooms, Bob described searching for truffles in the Kalahari with a group of San women. The women had an uncanny ability to find truffles in traces of moisture held within tiny, hidden cracks. Bob, who was raised as a farm boy and hunter, failed to find a single truffle while the women filled bag after bag. Here was a relic of the depth and potential of the hunting-gathering spirit. Yet returning to the relocation settlement was like walking into a squall of toxic rain. Alcohol, prostitution—and no more hunting or gathering.

Bob's writings describe the economic details: "Desperation lures young San women/girls to men with money. They charge 50 pula ($10) for sex with a condom and 200 pula ($40) without a condom." Then there is the funeral he attended:

> (It was a) burial near D'Kar of a young woman and her boyfriend. They were living together. He went to a party, got drunk, and slept with another woman, who is HIV positive. When he returned his girlfriend refused to sleep with him until he got tested. He broke her neck and then hanged himself.

The back-story behind these scenes of substance abuse, violence and prostituted aboriginal girls and women is one that has played itself out repeatedly the world over. The colonizers arrived in territories new to them and claimed lands and resources for themselves and their monarchs, stealing everything that mattered to the indigenous people inhabiting the area—forests, fish, animals, land, water, children—degrading women and imposing new systems of governance.

To address "the Indian problem" in Canada, the government adopted a policy of forced assimilation. The state relocated indigenous people away from their land, confined them into settlements with inadequate housing and no access to traditional food sources, criminalized cultural practices such as potlatches and dances, and systematically removed children from their homes. Agents of the church and state—ministers, social workers, priests, the police— marched into native houses to judge and condemn child-rearing practices and take children away to residential schools—government-sponsored institutions created to first dehumanize and then attempt to assimilate them. Between 1884 and 1996, one hundred and fifty thousand indigenous children in Canada were tracked down systematically, taken from their families, taught they were inferior, punished for speaking their own languages and forbidden to go home. Displaced from the land. Physically abused. Stripped of family connections.

So it was no surprise that I had encountered scenes near our home that resembled what Bob had witnessed in the Kalahari. I had walked back alleys in Whitehorse, Yukon, that were littered with needles and booze bottles, the stench of urine at every corner, the ghosts of displaced hunter-gatherers aimlessly wandering in an effort to find their way back to the land. In Vancouver's Downtown Eastside, I had seen the ghosts of just about every First Nation from Canada converging into nowhereness. But for the most part, all this was largely abstract to me, a problem that perhaps could be solved intellectually. It was not until Terry Jack came along that my subconscious cracked, even if just a little.

Twyla Bella, you met Terry Jack when we lived in the Yukon. During late August and early September of 2006, he would drive to our place in his pickup truck with a cooler of freshly caught sockeye salmon from his traditional territory, that of the Taku River Tlingit. It was a fantastic time of year, when the low bush cranberries were ripe for the picking, grouse and moose hunting season were unrolling, and the deep blue sky of frosty mornings contrasted against the reds, yellows and oranges of willows, dwarf birch and poplars in fall colour. During his fish deliveries, Terry indulged me by answering questions about his traditional territory, about the grizzly bears that fed on migrating salmon, the possibility of me visiting his fishing camp someday.

We moved south later that year and—perhaps out of shame for abandoning a land we had forged a connection with over fourteen years—I could not bring myself to tell Terry we were leaving. Bad move. Once south, I saw myself as the privileged white guy who had left when it was convenient, leaving behind the disposable Indian who had fulfilled a brief fling with Wild West romanticism. Yet that was not me, at least not entirely, and Terry had to know.

I asked Yukon friends about a postal address for Terry. Their reply was quick, providing the mailing address for the band office, along with depressing news. Terry—in a haze of drugs and alcohol—had beaten his wife, badly, and was in jail.

On January 1, 2007, I wrote a letter:

> Hi Terry,
> This is Alejandro, from Kilometre 3 on the Annie Lake Road. My family had got to know you this summer and fall through your fish business. You might remember my two-year-old daughter, Twyla Bella. We have fond memories of interacting with you, hearing about the Taku River salmon and your experiences hunting moose for the community. One thing I regret not telling you during your fish-selling visits is that, for many reasons, we were about to move to Bowen Island, on the coast of southern British Columbia, near Vancouver. So I am writing you from there, where I am starting to do my own Chinook fishing and crabbing.
>
> Through Matt and Kim, from the Carcross Road, I learned about how recent troubles sent you to jail. I was greatly saddened to hear about this. All I really want to do with this letter is send you good energy,

hoping that when you get out of jail you return to the Taku River, where the flowing waters can give you the healing you need, helping you resolve the troubles that put you where you are now, and giving you the strength to pursue the hunting and fishing spirit that has given great meaning to your life and that of your people.

Wishing you healing,
Alejandro

I mailed the letter, feeling some relief in my attempt to make up for the cowardice of my unannounced departure. Yet the feeling was short-lived. A couple of months later, an envelope arrived from the Yukon. The sender was Lois Moorcroft, our dear friend and former neighbour—the sort you ski over to visit when it is thirty-five below Celsius because you want warm conversation. Lois, a champion of the rights of women and aboriginal people in the North, had been working with the Taku River Tlingit First Nation. Inside her envelope was my unopened letter to Terry, and a message that she was returning it because it had been left on the post office notice board for several weeks.

And yes, Terry was still in prison.

Twyla Bella, around that time I dreamt that I was hunting moose with a partner. Who that partner was, I do not know. A moose cow with two calves appeared, heading towards me. I raised the rifle, ready to shoot. Why I would dream about shooting a cow with two calves, beats me. An instant before I shot, a man mounted on the cow appeared. Who it was, I cannot say for sure. I fired. Next thing I knew there were no moose in sight, and the man I had wounded was on the ground, being beaten on the head by my hunting partner with the butt of his rifle—presumably to put him out of his misery. I told my partner to stop, carried the injured man over my shoulder and began a silent journey towards, I now surmise, some form of medical help. But the journey and its outcome escape my awareness; I must have woken up around then.

WHATEVER THE DREAM MEANT (and I do have some ideas, ask me some day), I knew that Terry's dark behaviour and similar acts of violence by other Canadian aboriginals were the baggage of colonial violence and the mistreatment of seven generations of children at residential schools. I also knew that things were unlikely to improve until the encroachment of industrial developments and urbanization stopped taking wildlife and other traditional resources away from indigenous people. I have witnessed that encroachment in many places, from southern Chile to the Yukon.

Back in the winter of 1998, the Council of Yukon First Nations and the Yukon government jointly commissioned me to study a population of woodland caribou known as the Southern Lakes Herd. The work entailed snow-tracking the caribou on foot to reconstruct from their trails the sorts of habitats they used and the species of lichens that they fed on. We hoped to gain insight into the extent to which rural subdivisions and other developments around Whitehorse, the Yukon's capital and only city, might be hindering the recovery of the Southern Lakes Herd from over-hunting.

For centuries, the herd had been a major source of spiritual and physical nourishment for the Carcross/Tagish people, in whose traditional territory I was conducting the study. Stories handed down through oral tradition recalled a landscape characterized by "whole mountainsides moving with caribou." Yet all that began to change with the Klondike gold rush of 1898, which brought more than thirty thousand fortune seekers from faraway to the Yukon. The number of non-native people in the area surged again during the construction of the Alaska Highway in the 1940s. Many newcomers hunted caribou themselves, and professional market hunters came along to supply game meat to those who didn't. The shooting rampages were spectacular. Caribou habitats also began to change through land development and the suppression of natural fires that regenerate lichens, the woodland caribou's staple food. Yukon government biologists estimated in 1992 that the Southern Lakes herd had reached an all-time low of about a thousand animals. By then, non-aboriginals already were prohibited from hunting the herd and natives were exercising a self-imposed hunting ban. With the hunting pressure off, wildlife managers could turn their attention to the habitat issues that studies like mine were trying to unravel. Around this time, the Southern Lakes Caribou Recovery Program was born of aboriginal leadership and sympathetic biologists working in the community. It was a great opportunity for native and non-native neighbours to talk to each other and recognize a common goal in reviving the herd. I was proud to be contributing to that effort.

As I plodded through the snow, following tracks in the reverse direction of the animals' travel so that I would not catch up with the caribou and alter their behaviour, I alternated between excitement and pessimism. Inside mature forests of lodgepole pine and white spruce, I would encounter vast areas in which the animals had followed tightly turning sinuous pathways while digging through the snow and down to the ground, feasting on terrestrial lichens like the coral-like *Cladina mitis* and the leafier *Cetraria islandica*. This evidence of happy feasting reminded me of a morning in which Gail and I had woken up inside our cabin and watched a dozen woodland caribou through our bedroom window. The animals had lingered within view for the next six hours, resting and feeding, undisturbed on the meadow and forest edges that surrounded our home.

These behaviours contrasted with the straight tracks that crossed developed habitats, where lichens had been destroyed or that did not offer safe distances from people, road traffic and dogs. Here the caribou had travelled fast. With Whitehorse and its rural surroundings growing, it was hard to imagine that the Carcross/ Tagish people would be able to resume their traditional hunt of woodland caribou any time soon.

"We are seeing more caribou in the valley," Lois told me recently, and I was indeed pleased to hear that, seventeen years after my study, the animals were still there in our old neighbourhood, even showing signs of the possibility that they might bounce back. But the curse of being an ecologist is that I cannot ignore the bigger picture. As much as I would like to say that the long-term prospects for caribou have improved, I cannot.

Ecologists Glenn Yannic and Steeve Côté at Université Laval in Quebec, along with international colleagues, recently analyzed the genetic and environmental history of caribou and reindeer in Eurasia and North America. ("Caribou" and "reindeer" are different names for the same species, *Rangifer tarandus*. The common name depends on locale: caribou in North America, reindeer in Eurasia.) Their work reconstructed how climate variation altered habitats, causing the species to expand and contract its range during the last twenty-one thousand years. Once they understood how these cause-and-effect relationships operated back in time, they used computer models to travel into the future, projecting changes to habitats and caribou distributions in response to climate change. The analysis produced beautiful graphs and ugly results. It predicted that North American populations of caribou are likely to splinter, shrink and then vanish from 89 percent of their current distribution within the next sixty years.

Upon reading those findings, my thoughts turned to Art Johns, a Carcross/Tagish elder with unparalleled commitment to conservation and the rights of native subsistence hunters. I first met Art when he was in his sixties, at the start of my caribou study. He had a job that he loved: patrolling his traditional territory to ensure poachers and illegal developers were not messing with wildlife. Nobody else alive had a better on-the-ground understanding of the Southern Lakes Herd, and he wanted to make sure that my study would do the right thing. So he hunted me down and took me for a ride in his old Land Cruiser. We spent the day looking at caribou tracks, touring places I would be foolish to omit from my study. After that, Art made a point of swinging by my home office when he was in the neighbourhood, and I always dropped by to consult him whenever fieldwork took me near his home by Tagish Lake.

Art is now in his eighties. I confess that I have not been in touch with him for years, which is my loss, but I hear that he is very much alive. Art was born before the Southern Lakes Caribou Herd hit the bottom of the barrel. So he grew up hunting close to home with his father, the legendary outfitter Johnny Johns, experiencing the joys of forest and tundra food. I may never see Art again and, if I ever do, it will be tough. The encounter would remove all abstraction from those beautiful graphs depicting a future world diminished by the absence of caribou and the loneliness of a hunting culture that has lost one of its dearest relatives. Bearing the weight of that knowledge in the presence of Art would be heartbreaking. I would not know what to say.

I wish I could say that traditional fishing cultures of the coast face lesser challenges than their inland relations. But that would be untrue.

"DON'T SCREW UP OR there will be no feast," said Ernie Mason of the Kitasoo/Xai'Xais First Nation, between bouts of laughter as he slowly reeled in the huge halibut he had hooked. "Or I might break a leg," I added. Ernie is a big man, with an even bigger heart and a zeal for life that spreads anywhere he goes. But at that moment, I could not share his giddiness. I was tense as I gripped a gaff and stood, squeezed between twin outboard engines and the transom, on the narrow swim grid at the stern of the *Ci-du*, our twenty-six-foot research boat. We were near Laredo Channel, on the Central Coast of British Columbia. Ernie's wife, Sandie Hankewich, skilfully piloted the boat, keeping us from drifting with the strong current while holding their one-year-old daughter, Jesse, in her arms. Finally, the ghostly shape of the halibut became visible through the clear water while it was still at least ten metres deep. I tensed even more, visualizing the moves I would soon have to perform. Ernie directed the fish towards me as I leaned as far as I dared over the side of the boat. When the halibut's head was just about to reach the surface, but before it could break that surface and start thrashing, I went for it. The gaff's hook sank into the head and I used all of my weight and leg power to sprint backwards, dragging the halibut aboard and praying to every deity I could think of that I would not overshoot and hurl myself off the edge behind me.

I managed to halt my momentum at the right spot, but a happy ending was not yet in sight. Now I was stuck within the confines of the narrow platform, my right leg jammed between the halibut's thrashing body and the transom. Things got somewhat less pleasant when the gaff's hook pierced the far side of the fish's head and began digging into my entrapped foot. Laughing at my little situation, Ernie handed me another gaff, and I quickly used its blunt end to deliver three lethal blows to the halibut's head. With major injuries and lost feasts narrowly averted, I joined Ernie in his laughter.

We had caught the halibut on the way back to Klemtu, the Kitasoo/Xai'Xais village where Ernie and his family lived, after a day of conducting biological dive surveys. For several days we had been taking advantage of a prolonged period of calm waters, diving shoals and submerged pinnacles, often far offshore on the west coast of Aristazabal Island, all in between sightings of humpback whales, sea otters and Steller's sea lions. To say that I was delighted to be there would be a major understatement.

Nineteen years before, in 1994, Gail and I had kayaked through this area, exploring the traditional territories of the Haisla, Gitga'at, Kitasoo/Xai'Xais and Heiltsuk First Nations. For five weeks, we had lived largely from the fish we caught and the berries we picked, cooking on campfires and sleeping under an open sky or a tarp. We had drifted through tidal rapids, sat quietly inside old-growth forests, collapsed on sandy beaches after long crossings, and encountered the fresh tracks of wolves on many shores. When the shoreline had been too cliffy, we had slept on offshore rocks that were barely flat and wide enough for our sleeping bags, using driftwood logs jammed above the tide line as bridges between our "bedroom" and adjacent "kitchen" rocks. The journey had shaped Gail and me in ways that still influence the life we continue to live together.

Ever since, I had hoped for the opportunity to reconnect with these territories. Now that I was working with Ernie and Sandie, I carried the same nautical charts that Gail and I had used and annotated during our journey, so I could recognize, in detail, the campsites we had used and the shorelines and open waters we had paddled. Major landmarks of my life had gone full circle.

During June of 2013, about a month and a half before I began working with Ernie and Sandie, the Central Coast Indigenous Resource Alliance, a marine stewardship organization formed by the four First Nations of British Columbia's Central Coast—Heiltsuk, Kitasoo/Xai'Xais, Nuxalk and Wuikinuxv—had hired me as an ecologist. The nations knew that the combined effects of climate change, ocean acidification and fisheries were changing the oceans. Their tradition, in which all species are relatives living in interconnection, already gave them a profound understanding of what was going on. The only reason they needed someone like me was to come up with the numbers and technical language needed to negotiate with federal and provincial governments for marine protected areas and fishery closures.

So I was back in paradise, doing what I love. As if to drive that point home, within moments of arriving in Klemtu to start the fieldwork I had watched a twelve-year-old girl catch a coho salmon from the dock. Other kids giggled nearby, casting their own lures into the concentric circles that dozens of leaping and splashing coho had just made on the water surface. The sight of these kids having such fun, catching delicious wild foods within view of their homes, made me forget that I was there to analyze signs that paradise could be in real trouble. But it didn't take long before salmon reminded me why I was there.

Ernie works as a scientific diver and field technician with the Kitasoo Fisheries Program. Every couple of weeks during late summer, he counts the number of salmon spawning in creeks. I had arrived in Klemtu on the eve of one of these counts. The next morning we were travelling through a two-hundred-metre-deep fjord towards the Kynoch River. As we zoomed past cliffs that rose hundreds of metres straight out of the sea, Ernie pointed to pictographs that marked ledges where the remains of ancestors had been laid to rest in the old days. We anchored at the head of the fjord, where two biologists contracted by Canada's Department of Fisheries and Oceans were waiting for us. From there we all walked together up the Kynoch River valley, sometimes wading in the water, sometimes walking the sand and gravel bars. The meadow at the estuary was lush and vibrant. Fresh grizzly tracks covered the sandbars. Old-growth forest lined the river where thousands of pink salmon, a few hundred chum and coho and a handful of sockeye were busy reproducing and dying in the clear water.

The morning fog had cleared and the bright sunshine turned hot. I was enjoying the warmth and the sight of glaciers and granite ridges sparkling in the sun, but not without feeling a little guilty. As they counted salmon, my three companions kept muttering that this second consecutive month without rain was nothing short of eerie. "Here we go again," I thought to myself, but not unsympathetically. En route to this place that morning, Ernie had talked about the lack of rain as he pointed to shrinking waterfall after shrinking waterfall, expounding on how thin ribbons of water had replaced the booming falls that should still be here, even this late in summer. After all, this was supposed to be a temperate rainforest.

In the early 1990s, after more than a decade of studying the structure and function of temperate rainforests along the coasts of Alaska and Chile, ecologist Paul Alaback came up with an explicit definition of these biomes. For temperate rainforests to maintain their characteristics, which include moist-loving species of trees that grow to tremendous size, they need a minimum of 1.4 metres of annual precipitation, and at least 10 percent of that precipitation must occur during summer. Critically, most summer days have to remain cool and cloudy, rarely exceeding sixteen degrees Celsius, and forest fires must be extremely rare. This definition matched my own personal experiences of the British Columbia coast during the 1980s and '90s, when clear hot days had been a precious gift, not something to be taken for granted.

But things sure were different as we kept walking up the Kynoch River. The heat climbed into the twenties, reminding me that these formerly exceptional conditions were becoming the new normal. As if on cue, Ernie and his salmon-counting colleagues started talking about how Klemtu residents now worry about forest fires. In the many thousands of years that the Central Coast peoples had lived here, this had been an unimaginable fear, until recent decades. Next in order were exclamations about the river's low water levels and increased algal cover. And not to forget, the river's temperature that day had reached seventeen degrees Celsius, near the edge of very stressful conditions for salmon stocks adapted to the cool conditions that have characterized this area for many centuries.

I could not stop thinking how the hotter and drier trends matched global warming predictions. If they continue, these trends will end temperate rainforests as we know them, and transform the web of life that depends on salmon into something entirely different.

In coastal British Columbia and Alaska, grizzly bears and wolves feed in the late summer and fall on spawning salmon, abandoning partially eaten carcasses and depositing their feces and urine away from streams. Other species, such as eagles and seabirds, scavenge the carcasses of spawned-out salmon. In the process, salmon indirectly provide marine nutrients to terrestrial plants, to the point that years with productive salmon runs correlate to pulses in the growth of temperate rainforest trees. The carcasses also feed detritivores, animals such as beetles and other insects that feed on decaying animal matter. Even if salmon continue to use some of the streams, data from Alaska already warns that high stream temperatures in late summer could cause salmon to spawn earlier in the season and for shorter windows of time. This would disrupt the seasonal rounds that salmon-eating species have learned to expect over many generations, shortening that pulse of biological productivity that defines the entire ecosystem.

It was not hard to imagine that wherever creeks might become too low and warm for salmon to spawn, the forest and many of its inhabitants would go hungry. Ernie's people and other Central Coast nations would be bound to experience the same hunger; in this age of grocery stores they would not starve literally, but they certainly would spiritually. That erosion of spirituality is the last thing you want to wish on First Nation communities trying to get back on their feet after the residential school era. And given the tendency for native communities to consume junk food in the absence of wild foods, a drop in their health would add to the insult.

And the economic impact would be brutal. Klemtu has become world-renowned for its local business that guides visitors to view bears at places like the Kynoch River. The business employs forty of Klemtu's 340 residents, as guides, boat captains and in other capacities. The potential economic picture that emerges from too much heat in the coastal rainforest looks something like this. More climate change means fewer salmon and therefore fewer bears at streams, which means fewer jobs for a First Nation community that—during prior times of severe unemployment—has experienced weekly suicides.

TWYLA BELLA, MY FIRST visit to the Kynoch River triggered many thoughts about how the loss of biodiversity hurts cultural diversity, and therefore is inseparable from the rights of many people. Especially in the context of climate change and industrial fisheries. Remember the Bella Coola River, a few mountain ranges east of the Kynoch, where you, Gail and I swam not long ago? That river is the lifeline of the Nuxalk Nation not only because of salmon, but also because of eulachon, a species of smelt crucial to the identity, history, food and medicine of the Nuxalkmc. Like salmon, eulachon are anadromous; they spawn in rivers but spend most of their lives at sea. Nuxalk fisheries always have focused on the Bella Coola River, where eulachon runs were strong throughout most of the twentieth century. Back then, the abundance was extraordinary. Imagine the "stink boxes" used to ferment eulachon into oil, each holding five to eight tons of fish. Generation after generation of Nuxalkmc filled a great many of these boxes every year. That is, until the 1990s, when what had been a subtle decline accelerated and eulachon collapsed throughout central and southern British Columbia. The timing of the declines paralleled the rise of trawl fisheries that target shrimp or groundfish but capture eulachon as bycatch. At the same time, climate change has been altering conditions that influence growth and survival of eulachon. So the declines might relate to a synergistic effect of trawl bycatch and climate change. The research to investigate this has yet to happen. Meanwhile, to say that the declines have devastated the Nuxalk and other First Nations would be an understatement. My colleague, Wilfred Dawson, describes:

> I remember fishing right over here, one of the last runs that the Bella Coola River had, not realizing… the fish were there every year and then all of a sudden for them not to appear in the numbers that they had is devastating. It was one of our main medicines, one of the big things we have lost. Our health has been affected by the loss of the species.

AFTER THAT DAY AT the Kynoch River, my teamwork with Ernie, Sandie and other Klemtu residents became all about studying the abundance, distribution and body sizes of my favourite inhabitants of rocky reefs. As you probably guessed from my earlier stories, I am talking about species belonging to the genus *Sebastes*—collectively known as rockfish—and lingcod. These fish play a major role in the culture and economy of British Columbia's coastal First Nations, yet are fished hard by sports and commercial fishers.

Fisheries target the largest and oldest individuals. This is bad news for all species but particularly hard on the many rockfish which live sixty to 120 years or more, and especially tough on those species that do not start reproducing until they are ten to twenty years or older. For one thing, many rockfish caught within their first ten years of life die without ever reproducing. Another factor is that rockfish mothers produce more offspring as they age. A vermillion rockfish, for instance, produces *only* fifty to a hundred thousand larvae a year when it starts reproducing—but if it manages to evade fishers and predators long enough, it will produce more than two and half million larvae per season during the last years of its natural lifespan. Every time a batch of baby rockfish goes out into the world, odds are that only a tiny proportion will make it to adulthood and reproduction. In this game of probabilities, mothers that put out only thousands of larvae per year rather than millions—and which get to live only a portion of their natural lifespan—may not contribute enough recruits to sustain a population. On top of their higher productivity, older rockfish mothers also produce better offspring. Rockfish larvae are born with a built-in nutrient supply in the form of an oil globule. As rockfish mothers age, their larvae have larger globules, which enable them to survive better and grow faster than larvae born to younger mothers. No matter how you slice it, catching mothers that are large and old—which commercial and sports fishers are allowed to do under current regulations— promotes rockfish disaster.

And let's not forget about lingcod. Recall that this species lives shorter lives (only about thirty-five years, at most) and reproduces faster than long-lived rockfish. In principle, these characteristics make them less vulnerable to overfishing. The problem is that lingcod are easy to catch and fillet, and their meat is delicious. So fishers target them that much harder, to the point that many lingcod populations have plenty of their own troubles.

To study the status of rockfish and lingcod populations, our crew dove to count fish and study their habitats, and used fishing gear to sample fish from depths beyond the reach of divers. (The study is still ongoing, and has expanded by using towed video cameras to survey very deep waters, and by sampling the catch of native fishers who use groundlines with hundreds of baited hooks to supply the village with traditional food.)

After Klemtu, I travelled to the territories of the Heiltsuk, Wuikinuxv and Nuxalk First Nations, where I joined locals in more studies of rockfish and lingcod. Over the course of the late summer and early fall, we sampled thousands of square kilometres of the Central Coast, covering inside and outside waters and a very wide range of depths. The good news is that we established the methodology for a long-term monitoring program of rockfish and lingcod to be carried out by the First Nations themselves, and in the process found several areas important to long-lived rockfish.

The bad news is that we did not find very many big fish. In particular, I was blown away that our sampling recorded very few lingcod longer than eighty-five centimetres. Based on historical data and my prior experience in Haida Gwaii, I had expected to encounter a substantial number of lingcod that were well over ninety centimetres long. In the absence of overfishing, we would have been sure to find many "bucket heads"—breeding females with lengths exceeding 120 centimetres and jaws wide enough to swallow a human head. But as Frank Johnson, former chief of the Wuikinuxv First Nation, told me one September day while we drank tea at his home, the last "bucket head" he knew of had been caught thirty years earlier. The absence of large lingcod and the scarcity of very large rockfish suggested that overfishing was already making deep marks not only on individual species but on the whole ecosystem, by eliminating the largest top predators, which contribute to overall species diversity by affecting the behaviour and numbers of smaller predators.

Whatever fishing impact our data reflected was, arguably, the smallest of the ocean's troubles. As long as the political will exists, it is entirely possible to stop or modify harmful fisheries (though finding that political will is a whole other story). Even long-lived species of rockfish can recover their former age structure if we stop fishing them for several decades. As I will soon tell you through other stories, what worries me most is that once unleashed, changes to the chemistry and temperature of the oceans that harm marine life are not so easy to reverse.

Good thing that all of my colleagues from the Central Coast have such a wicked sense of humour.

TWYLA BELLA, I WANTED you to know these stories so you could begin to see that social justice and the conservation of the biosphere are inseparable. With no territory to hunt, gather and fish in, traditional subsistence cultures face extinction. This loss of cultural diversity impoverishes the world as much as the loss of biological diversity.

The day Ernie hooked that big halibut, we arrived at Klemtu as daylight was fading. Kids were still catching coho salmon in the late twilight, parents and grandparents hanging around with them. Ernie and I filleted the halibut on the dock, making everyone present, already in a festive mood, even more upbeat. Ernie was excited about the big slabs of fish he was about to deliver to his parents, and my mouth watered as I anticipated the smell of fresh halibut cooking.

It was hard to acknowledge that we were inside a spreading crack of climate change and overfishing. But that is exactly where we were. A cynic will tell you that I was witnessing the last of a good ride, but I have a different interpretation.

What I am about to tell you originates in the prisons of Greater Vancouver, where many inmates are indigenous people who have lost their connection to the land. As a modern dance choreographer known for her ability to express complex issues through her art form, your mother, Gail, was invited to work on a project that used dance to express concepts of restorative justice. The work took her into those prisons, where she guided inmates into moving their bodies as an expression of their life stories. In the process, she saw the spectrum of the human spirit move before her very eyes. One day she came home and distilled what she had learned into these words: "Spirituality is more than a set of beliefs; it is a set of intentions."

The moment I heard them, I knew Gail's words originated not only in prisons, but also on the sandy beaches and rainforests of the Central Coast, where so many of our own intentions came to life two decades ago. At the end of the day, Gail and I know that the indigenous people we work with consider bears, wolves, fish, whales and other creatures their relatives. That is their ancient tradition. When you live within that cosmology, giving up on the ocean and forest, or each other, is a notion that cannot exist.

Love,
Pops

CHAPTER 6

Ever Try to De-acidify an Ocean?

Dear Twyla Bella,

Artists, poets and musicians make us feel, viscerally, how people destroy what they do not understand. Logic and observation led pioneer ecologist E.O. Wilson to conclude: "If people don't know, they don't care. If they don't care, they don't act."

Whether you feel it in "Hieroglyphic Stairway"—the poem by Drew Dellinger that committed me to writing these letters for you—or visualize it in the beauty of data, the song remains the same. Scientists are critical to the present and future of the biosphere and humanity, but if—and only if—we are free to communicate our findings to the voting public.

Galileo did not have the right to speak out. Scientists in totalitarian regimes of today still lack it. And now, incredibly, some of Canada's top scientists have lost that right.

That is not the Canada I came to. Rewind the tape to 1983. I was a young immigrant, ecstatic that my family had gained entry into the country. We all had mixed feelings; we love our birth country of Mexico and were sad to leave it, yet we looked forward to being part of Canada's open-minded and science-loving spirit. The tape runs forward and not all turns out to be as advertised. Still, for the next twenty-three years

Canada remained a damn good place, ruled by governments that, imperfect as they may have been, were not obsessed with burying science.

Fast-forward the tape to 2006. Stephen Harper's newly elected Conservative Party hit the ground, pounding punches in all directions. Almost immediately, the Conservatives began to implement one of their many Machiavellian tactics that aim to turn Canada into a petro-state: downgrade science as irrelevant to the decision-making process. In the nine years since, federal scientists have seen their programs slashed or buried. Those who manage to hang on to their jobs are forbidden to speak about their findings to the media or the public.

Federal scientists publishing research in *Science* or *Nature* with strong implications for policies on climate change or other environmental crises are not even allowed to write a press release about their findings. Presenters at the 2012 International Polar Year conference in Montreal had government "handlers" shadowing their every move so that they might not slip into the unpatriotic act of speaking to journalists about energy policies that affect the melting Arctic and Earth's climate. These scenes are not from a prequel to George Orwell's *1984*. They are the true experiences of top-notch scientists in the Medieval Canada of today.

A parallel tactic to muzzling scientists is to ignore them even if they do speak. After Harper gutted Canada's Fisheries Act in 2012, stripping away the legal obligation to protect fish habitat, Jeffrey A. Hutchings, president of the Canadian Society for Ecology and Evolution, formally asked the fisheries minister for the science justifying that decision. Hutchings, a distinguished ecologist and fishery scientist, never received a direct answer because, of course, there isn't one.

The Fisheries Act was gutted so that thousands of stream crossings by proposed fossil fuel pipelines would not trigger legally mandated environmental assessments and slow down corporate agendas. Since being rudely ignored by a government that hates data, Hutchings and his colleague John Post have put some numbers to the cost of Medieval governance. Without the old version of the Fisheries Act—which protected fish for 144 years before Harper gutted it—extractive industries are free to trample, legally, over the habitat of 80 percent of freshwater fish species currently at risk of extinction in Canada. No wonder that, unlike many leaders of modern democracies, Harper has never appointed a science advisor, not even a fake one.

Canadian resource extraction policies were certainly imperfect before Harper's 2006 election. Havoc did exist then too. The difference is that, back then, Canadian governments did not actively seek to convert the country into a petro-state where fossil fuels rule at the expense of science and democracy.

The downgrading of science by the Canadian government is a big deal, not just to Canadians but to all world citizens, because much of the loss of evidence-based decision-making—as in the gutting of the Fisheries Act and the potential watering down of the Species at Risk Act—is about fast-tracking new infrastructure for the extraction and export of fossil fuels. If built, that new infrastructure will commit us to many more decades of emissions and a future of perilous climate change.

That is why colleagues and I have, reluctantly, become neo-traditional scientists: grounded in the traditions of the scientific method and objectivity, yet increasingly engaged in the politics that will make or break our future. This is not the classic role of scientists, who, until recently, were trained to remain apolitical and let others figure out the societal implications of their data. But those times are no more. Either the proverbial lab coats hit the streets with protest, en masse, or your generation will be deprived of a decent future.

A LETTER ARRIVED ON May 1, 2012. Unannounced and directed to somebody else, its message was precisely what I needed. Forwarded by NASA climatologist James Hansen to subscribers of his email list, the letter was addressed to Warren Buffet, the famous magnate and owner of BNSF trains. It read:

Dear Mr. Buffett:

We want to inform you that on Saturday, May 5th, from midnight to midnight, we intend to prevent BNSF coal trains from passing through White Rock, British Columbia to deliver their coal to our coastal ports for export to Asia. We have chosen May 5th to take this action because it has been designated an International day of action by 350.org, with the theme "Connecting the Dots." We can't think of a more important connection to emphasize than the one between burning coal and putting our collective future at risk.

We are a group of citizens in British Columbia, Canada who are deeply concerned about the risk of runaway climate change. There is a broad scientific consensus that we must begin to sharply reduce greenhouse gas emissions this decade to avoid climate change becoming irreversible. At the same time, governments and industry are eager to *increase* the production and export of fossil fuels, the very things that will ensure climate change *does* get worse.

These two things are irreconcilable, and since we can't dispute the scientific findings or change the laws of nature, those of us who care about the future must do what we can to reduce the production, export and burning of fossil fuels—especially coal.

Since we know what is at stake we feel a moral obligation to do what we can to help prevent this looming disaster. On Saturday May 5th that means stopping your coal trains from reaching our ports.

Our actions will be peaceful, non-violent, and respectful of others. There will be no property destruction. We are striving to be the best citizens we can. We will stand up for what we believe is right and conduct ourselves with dignity.

We acknowledge that this action is taking place on unceded Coast Salish territory.

Sincerely,
British Columbians for Climate Action
stopcoal.ca

It took me a while to convince myself that the letter was not written by a bunch of hockey-riot-type yahoos in search of a little fun. In retrospect, I was freaked—looking for the hair trigger that would allow me to dismiss the whole thing. Nice try. The sobriety and good intentions of the writers could not have been more obvious.

I suppose that my feelings were understandable. I had never been arrested before, and my inexperience equated with fear of things turning ugly. But every time I read and reread the letter I got closer to throwing caution to the wind until, by dawn on May 5, my friend Lynne Quarmby—who at the time chaired the Department of Molecular Biology and Biochemistry at Simon Fraser University—and I sat at the back of a public bus, wondering whether we had just volunteered to become shark bait. Despite our fears, the two of us had committed to crossing a new threshold because the standard democratic channels were proving inadequate as tools to end inaction against climate change. For months the words "civil disobedience" had been uttered with rising frequency in conversations among our colleagues. Many of us had been inspired by James Hansen, who had led by example the previous year when he got himself arrested in front of the White House to protest the proposed Keystone Pipeline that would carry bitumen from Alberta to the United States. That had been his third arrest in three years: the previous two involved civil disobedience against the mining of coal. There was no precedent for a senior NASA scientist taking that stance; his willingness to incur such risks was a signal of how dire the climate crises would soon become if inaction continued.

The bus delivered Lynne and me to the train tracks while it was still morning. Coal trains remained notably absent for most of that day. The threat of a blockade disrupted the railway schedule, keeping several coal trains from crossing the U.S. border and, at some level, getting our point across to BNSF. The opportunity to strengthen that point was still to come.

Towards sunset, a 125-car coal train destined to release 26,000 tonnes of CO_2 into our atmosphere appeared in the distance, heading our way. Thirteen of us moved on to the tracks. Among us, a man in his eighties, several men in their sixties and seventies, and a few youngsters like myself and Lynne. As we waited, I told Mark Jaccard—a distinguished energy economist at Simon Fraser University and former member of the Intergovernmental Panel on Climate Change—that the announcement that he would participate in the blockade had sealed my decision to make a stand. Jaccard replied that, given what he knew about the climate crisis and the consequences of inaction, it was impossible for him not to be there. He was echoing sentiments shared by all thirteen of us on the tracks.

As we had hoped, the blockade turned out to be a peaceful act of science communication. The train slowed down and halted in front of us. Before arresting us, the police allowed us to speak to the media and observers about intergenerational justice and the millions of people already suffering from climate change. There were no hasty moves during the handcuffing or the ride in the paddy wagon. There was no property or personal damage. There were only carefully crafted ideas and deeply held convictions. Fellow protester Kevin Washbrook said it best: "[It] was a good day to be a Canadian citizen." Later, as we were released from jail, Jaccard wondered out loud whether the arrest would affect his ability to travel to meet with the U.S. Environmental Protection Agency, with which he was a consultant on renewable energy policies. Then he said something to the effect that, "You can forever come up with excuses, or you can get real and just do it."

But what had we really done?

After our arrest, the train had continued on its way, all that

CO_2 soon to be released into our atmosphere, encapsulating the paradox that I live with: I do not believe that my individual actions will change the world, yet I know that the world cannot change without our collective individual actions.

As I HINTED IN my earlier stories, the ocean absorbs a third of the CO_2 that we pump into the atmosphere, and consequently is becoming more acidic. The larvae of some species, from fishes to urchins to oysters, cannot tolerate this change in water chemistry, so populations of these life forms may be entering a downward spiral. Some of these species feed people directly. Others, like Antarctic krill, feed us at a more fundamental level—by keeping entire oceans alive. Antarctic krill have acid-intolerant larvae so—unless our energy policies change soon—they are predicted to go extinct within the next three centuries. Their extinction might not seem imminent, but the fact that it is even on the horizon warns of the unrecognizable world we could be heading into. Antarctic krill happen to support food webs that involve fish, seabirds, whales and seals; their demise could terminate most vertebrate species in today's southern oceans.

The problem of ocean acidification is inseparable from that of climate warming because the two processes feed each other in synergistic ways. For instance, as the oceans acidify, they increase the rate at which they release another greenhouse gas into the atmosphere: dimethylsulphide. Through this process, acidification could boost global warming 10 percent above that caused by CO_2 emissions. And as the oceans warm, marine phytoplankton—microscopic plants that produce half of the oxygen we breathe and remove half of the atmospheric CO_2 that is fixed into plant tissues—grow larger and ramp up their photosynthetic activity. At first, that sounds pretty good: more photosynthesis means less CO_2 in the atmosphere. The problem is that phytoplankton respond to warming by altering their individual cells in ways that demand more nitrogen to function. Because nitrogen abundance in the ocean varies geographically and over time, instances in which large numbers of phytoplankton cannot find enough nitrogen for photosynthesis could occur in the future. The potential result is what Jack A. Gilbert, a microbiologist at the Argonne National Laboratory in Illinois, calls "a catastrophic positive feedback loop," leading to more atmospheric CO_2 *and* more warming *and* more acidification *and* more CO_2 and...the loop continues, ad nauseam.

The ocean is where huge portions of humanity find most of their food, and where the majority of living things that occupy our planet originated and still live. To the fossil fuel industry and its political supporters, losing this foundation of life on Earth is a mere externality: collateral damage in the name of business.

WHICH IS WHY I ask myself, almost every day: Ever try to de-acidify an ocean?

The question haunts me because, unless the answer is "yes and it worked"—which of course it hasn't, and is unlikely to ever work—inquiries into the local impacts of pipelines, shipping terminals and other infrastructure for the transport of fossil fuels are a distraction from the imperative to leave most remaining fossil fuels in the ground.

Some think this position is a bit much, but others stand behind it. Writing in *Nature Climate Change*, Ronald Stouffer, a geophysicist with the National Oceanic and Atmospheric Administration in Princeton, invites readers to consider the following question: "Can you believe that the decisions you make today could continue to impact the climate 1,000 years from now?" In doing so, Stouffer erects an intellectual straw man for us to knock down and, in the process, get a grip on reality. That reality is that every bit of CO_2 that we emit today will affect the climate for the next thousand years or so. One reason is that the tremendous thermal mass of the oceans requires that long to fully absorb any heat increment that occurs in the atmosphere, and whatever warming the oceans take on exacerbates sea level rise and other nasty consequences of climate change. On top of that, two-thirds of the CO_2 that we emit today will spend decades to centuries warming up the atmosphere before the carbon cycle captures it back into plants, soils and—I hate to tell you—the ocean, but the remaining third will stay in the atmosphere, making a mess for a whole thousand years.

Yet these facts are not to be misconstrued into fatalism. Climatologists Damon Matthews at Concordia University and Susan Solomon at MIT point out that "Irreversible does not mean unavoidable." In a paper of that title published in *Science*, they argue that grounds for optimism are very much alive. If we were to cut down emissions, starting right now, the carbon cycle would remove enough CO_2 from the atmosphere in time to avert major climate disasters and without killing the oceans through acidification. And Susan Solomon is no Pollyanna. She is the lead author of the paper "Irreversible climate change due to carbon dioxide emissions," published in the *Proceedings of the National Academy of Science* and cited widely for its insights into the millennial permanence of CO_2 emissions. So when she tells us to stay positive *and* cut emissions, we should do exactly that.

These scientists mean what they say because we cannot count on technology to save the day. According to the American Physical Society, the current cost of removing CO_2 and other greenhouse gases from the atmosphere and capturing them underground is $7.3 trillion per gigatonne. (One gigatonne, or Gt, is a billion metric tonnes.) To continue with business as usual—emitting 52 Gt of carbon dioxide equivalents (CO_{2e}) per year, as we did in 2012—without increasing the concentration of atmospheric CO_2, we would have to spend $381.7 trillion, every year, in carbon capture and sequestration. Not even Wall Street would buy into that.

NOW THAT YOU KNOW these things, I can tell you what I really want say. To paraphrase the late American writer Gertrude Stein, a new pipeline is a new pipeline is a new pipeline. Building more of them—whether labelled "eco-friendly" or not—promotes global suicide. To show you what I mean, here is the story of another letter.

In March of 2013 I saw a posting for a job with the Smithsonian Conservation Biology Institute, which was seeking a "Conservation Biologist to provide expert advice in the design and implementation of a Biodiversity Monitoring and Assessment Program in Northern British Columbia, Canada." The job sounded cool and important. I was suited for it, knew northern British Columbia well and loved the idea of working there.

But there was a catch. The job focused on the *local* impacts of fossil fuel infrastructure while dissociating itself from the climate impacts of burning that fuel, and involved collaborating with the fossil fuel company. According to the posting, this was not a new thing for the Smithsonian:

> Guided by the principles of the Convention on Biological Diversity, the Smithsonian Conservation Biology Institute works with a selected group of oil and gas companies since 1996 to develop models designed to achieve conservation and sustainable development objectives while also protecting and conserving biodiversity, and maintaining vital ecosystem services that benefit both humans and wildlife.

Given that climate change is already diminishing global biodiversity and hampering the ecosystem services on which we all depend, the logic seemed inconsistent to me. But there was little time to ponder it. The application deadline had just passed and funding for my position with the Vancouver Aquarium Marine Science Centre was fizzling out. So I applied, hastily, figuring that I would deal with the issue later, if they ever got back to me.

Months went by without a word and I felt relieved, freed from choice. But all that changed with an email requesting a video interview as soon as possible. Using the legitimate excuse that I was on an intense field course, I managed to stall the interview by a week, which gave me some time to consult friends, do some reading and CO_{2e} calculations, and just wrap my mind and conscience around the whole thing. All this led to my letter to the Smithsonian, reproduced below in its entirety, sent the day before my scheduled interview.

7 May 2013
To Whom It May Concern:

I was pleased to find out last week that the Center for Conservation Education and Sustainability of the Smithsonian Conservation Biology Institute (SCBI) shortlisted me for an interview regarding the position of Conservation Biologist in Northern BC. I have great regard for SCBI, and at first I was delighted by the potential opportunities. In the last few days, however, I have reviewed the context of the position and have decided to withdraw my application. My reasons for doing so are based entirely on personal ethics. Let me explain.

According to the job description, the work would entail "research to study, understand, predict, and monitor the impact of infrastructure development projects on biodiversity and ecosystem services". In this case the infrastructure, to be built by Apache Canada Ltd, is to serve the export of Liquefied Natural Gas (LNG) and includes a plant, storage facility, marine on-loading facilities, and the 470-kilometre Pacific Trails Pipeline. On the positive side, it is good that the very high scientific standards of SCBI will help reduce the local impacts of the LNG infrastructure project. On the negative side, a sole focus on local impacts implicitly turns a blind eye to the severe climate impacts associated with the project.

According to their website, the Pacific Trails Pipeline will have a capacity of up to one billion cubic feet per day. When burnt, that amount of gas would release 19.9 million tonnes of CO_{2e} per year. Emissions generated during extraction, transport, processing, storing, and handling would be additional.

The impact on biodiversity and ecosystem services of releasing that much CO_{2e} into the atmosphere would, in my opinion, trump the accomplishments of any project focused on local impacts of infrastructure. For instance, Rogelj et al. (*Nature Climate Change* 2013, 3:405–12) estimate that to avoid the climate disasters that will occur if global temperatures rise more than two degrees Celsius above pre-industrial times, annual emissions must drop globally from 52 gigatonnes (Gt: billion metric tonnes) of CO_{2e} emitted in 2012 to 41-47 Gt by 2020. The Pacific Trails Pipeline would transport, *annually*, the equivalent of 0.04 percent of *total global emissions* generated in 2012. Although this proportion may, at first glance, seem small, the impact of greenhouse gases on the climate is cumulative and the Pacific Trails Pipeline would be adding emissions to those already produced by thousands of other existing pipelines. The construction of that project or any other new fossil fuel infrastructure, therefore, is the opposite of what should happen if we are to reduce the impacts of anthropogenic climate change on biodiversity and society.

I want to conclude by saying that I have great admiration and respect for SCBI. Having said that, I am stunned that SCBI is not taking a stronger stance against the climate and global impacts associated with new infrastructure for fossil fuel exports. While all sorts of arguments for socioeconomic and political compromises can be made, in the end it comes down to physics and chemistry, which know no compromise. The current concentration of atmospheric CO_2 is 398 parts per million (ppm) and rising at an average rate of 2 ppm/year. While LNG is a less dirty fuel than bitumen or coal, it is still a fossil fuel that only contributes to the rise in greenhouse gas emissions, taking us farther away from 350 ppm, the upper limit of "safe" CO_2 concentrations. Emissions have to go down, and building new infrastructure for fossil fuels is not going to make that happen.

So please accept the withdrawal of my application.

Respectfully,
Alejandro Frid

A day after sending my letter, journalist Stephen Leahy reported in *Desmog Canada* that methane leaks from the natural gas industry in British Columbia had been underestimated, and that numbers revised by Robert Howarth, a biogeochemist at Cornell University, added "nearly 25% to BC's carbon footprint: like adding 3 million cars." Two weeks later the Grantham Research Institute on Climate Change and the Environment at the London School of Economics released their *Unburnable Carbon* report, which points to the economic foolishness of building new infrastructure for fossil fuels that would lock us deeper into a carbon economy. Soon after, I read peer-reviewed evidence that fossil fuel corporations have been key players in the climate change denial industry.

Since then, I have learned that natural gas is mostly methane (85% or more) and no other fossil fuel surpasses its rate of methane emissions. This is terrible news. Although methane lasts only a few decades in the atmosphere, a lot less than CO_2, the global warming it produces over twenty years is 86 to 105 times greater than that produced by an equivalent mass of CO_2. We should all really care about this fact because it means that the short-term yet powerful warming caused by methane indirectly exacerbates long-term climate change by unleashing positive feedback loops, such as speeding up the release of greenhouse gases from the melting Arctic tundra and accelerating the loss of sea ice, which reflects solar radiation back into space. This is doubly bad news because the British Columbia government has launched an aggressive development program as well as a propaganda campaign that touts liquefied natural gas as a "climate solution," capitalizing on the fact that methane lasts for less time in the atmosphere than CO_2.

This campaign disseminates only selective pieces of information (read "lies"), includes hefty impact benefit agreements to entice the support of First Nations (read "bribes"), and is fundamentally flawed because it fails to account for the very severe and long-term climate impacts that methane causes indirectly. No wonder Robert Howarth warns that reducing methane emissions over the next fifteen to thirty-five years is critical if we are to avert severe runaway climate change disasters.

So I stand only firmer today on my decision to withdraw from my interview with the Smithsonian Institute.

I had sent my letter of withdrawal with no expectation of a substantive response. Accordingly, the reply was limited to "we appreciate your thoughts" and "best of luck in your future endeavours." Fair enough; the Smithsonian had signed on to a job interview for work they had already committed to, not an ethics debate.

But *I* wanted that debate. So I wrote about this experience in *Conservation Bytes*, an online publication read primarily by ecologists, where I asked the following question: "Is the long-term conservation of biodiversity and ecosystem services best served by working with the fossil fuel industry on local impacts or by boycotting industry collaborations that implicitly legitimize and endorse further growth of our carbon economy?" People did write their answers, some endorsing my actions, some not. Here is one example.

> Great discussion here: I would say—why not take the job and cause change/impact from within? They obviously saw something in you—and were willing to accept you. If we always decline to work with "industry"—then we are deliberately excluding ourselves from a process of improvement—from learning, and from providing our scientific knowledge to those systems that REALLY need our input. This is akin to refusing to work with the World Bank because they fund development projects—that of course destroy biodiversity. But brave people who took that

chance early on—have now created one of the
world's greatest funds for biodiversity work. Without
people willing to jump in and initiate change, the
Bank would never have learned.

My version is that this sort of reply—though well intended—
misses the point. I say this because I believe there is a distinction
between a project that creates new infrastructure for fossil fuel development versus one that merely logs, fishes or builds dams. Yes,
I used the word "merely" deliberately, because of the differences
in temporal and spatial scale of impact between these two kinds
of projects.

New infrastructure for fossil fuels is insanely expensive and the
associated profits are extraordinary. Once investors have footed the
bill, society commits to burning those fuels for many decades. Try
telling investors that their new multi-billion-dollar pipeline has to
run dry ahead of schedule to save the climate and, even if you are
a head of state, you will hear from their powerful lawyers. So a shift
towards a low-carbon economy is unlikely to even begin without
a moratorium on new infrastructure for fossil fuels. Without that
moratorium, the world could be four and half degrees warmer than
it was in pre-industrial times by 2100. With temperatures like that,
most local biodiversity that we were proud to conserve early in the
twenty-first century will be on pretty tenuous ground long before
2100.

An industrial logging, fishing or hydro project is a whole different beast, one that I am willing to consider being involved with.
For instance, I have partnered in the past with a mining company
in an effort to reduce its impact on mountain ungulates. Given a
stable climate, or at least one that has not gone berserk in response
to our carbon economy, logging, fishing and similar industries can
be managed in a way that fosters resilience at a scale of decades
(assuming politicians respond to the scientific recommendations).
I can work with that.

Now, I am not completely pigheaded about this. Some new
natural gas developments could, potentially, help bridge the tran-

sition from fossil fuels to renewable energies. But that argument is credible only if two of its assumptions are in fact true. The first is that politicians in power do not hate data and actively adjust policies in response to scientific advice. The second is that those same politicians actually believe in a transition to renewable energy, and have an overarching vision for the planned phase-out of fossil fuels, including retraining workers from those industries so that they can continue to make a decent living in a different occupation. Yet those assumptions are utterly false in the Medieval Canada of today. Until that changes, I am steering clear of industries that have blown the entire planet out of the Holocene—the geologic epoch that twelve thousand years ago brought the benign climate that allowed civilization to evolve—and whose impacts will stay for millennia.

Ever tried to de-acidify an ocean?

I WISH I COULD say that the ruffling of some Smithsonian feathers was my major saga for 2013, but that would be untrue. Instead, the blockbuster event of that year was all about king coal going crazy.

It was February when many of us learned that the port authority, Port Metro Vancouver, intended to convert the "green" city of Vancouver into North America's largest exporter of climate-destroying emissions. The Port began by allowing an existing shipping terminal to double its capacity to export metallurgical coal, which is used to make steel. Speaking on TV, a representative of the Mining Association of British Columbia praised the expansion, angelically wooing the public with a well-rehearsed script: "Steel-making coal in particular is in almost everything we touch." In other words, they implied, business is inflexible, never mind the climate. (I will return to this point in a moment.)

That was the warm-up. Next, the Port, accountable to the Harper Government and nobody else—which is the same as saying loyal to the coal industry and uninterested in the citizenry— created a façade of public consultation while trying to steamroll the approval of a new terminal on the Fraser River for the export of thermal coal, which is used to generate electricity. If built, that terminal would boost Vancouver's coal export capacity to fifty-five million tonnes per year, two-thirds more than it was in 2012. Burning that coal would produce about 105 million tonnes of carbon dioxide every year: 70 percent more than the entire province of British Columbia emitted in 2011.

Coal, whether used to generate electricity or make steel, has the greatest potential of all fossil fuels for disrupting Earth's climate. To avoid massive climate mitigation costs, 65 percent of the world's coal plants must shut down by 2020. Leading climate scientists have said so: building new coal infrastructure in the name of a sustainable economy is like using gasoline to put out a house fire.

So today I seethe in anger while a familiar Bruce Cockburn tune blares through my internal speakers:

If I had a rocket launcher, I'd make somebody pay

This is so avoidable. For those who consider the transition away from fossil fuels to non-carbon energy sources a pipe dream, here are some facts from the International Energy Agency a Paris-based intergovernmental organization dedicated to energy security. Global public subsidies in 2011 amounted to $523 billion to the fossil fuel industry but only $88 billion for renewable energies. Shift those figures around and we shall see who has been living in a pipe dream.

If I had a rocket launcher, I would not hesitate

And we can thin our diet of metallurgical coal. To be fair, the industry claim that the angelic stuff is in "almost everything we touch" has some truth, but one that deserves to be met with some rather fundamental questions. Like: *Must we really set our bar so low that only the same old destructive thing is possible?* And: *Can't the genius who invented walking do better?*

Julian Allwood, leader of the Low Carbon Materials Processing Group at the University of Cambridge, hints at the answers. For starters, his math shows that the global demand for metallurgical coal would drop by one-third if we did three rather obvious things: built buildings to last one to two hundred years (instead of fifty, as currently done in his native U.K.), stopped over-building cars and other products with way more steel than they need to perform, and behaved as if community matters. In Allwood's equations, community means this: We can get a lot more bang for the buck of each steel product if we shift from individual car or bike ownership to co-ops, and get into the habit of managing commercial buildings so that different users occupy the same space at different times. This may not be the all-American dream of stock-market-bubble-type freedom—free to burst, I suppose—but it may just be the sort of attitude that helps us stay human for a lot longer than we would otherwise. Thousands of city dwellers belonging to car and bike co-ops and shared-space arrangements already walk that talk, from New York to Vancouver and beyond—but we still have to make that the new normal, in as many far-flung places as possible. And there is one more thing that does not even require consumers to lift a finger. One-quarter of all steel is wasted during manufacturing, and the engineering capacity to turn that waste into actual product already exists. Implementing that capacity would lower consumption of metallurgical coal even more.

But the math that really gets me is this. Stanford engineer Mark Jacobson is among the many number crunchers showing that barriers to large-scale use of renewable energies are "primarily social and political, not technological or economic." And Mark Jaccard—that distinguished economist with paddy-wagon status—reminds us that "when the British Columbia government cancelled one natural gas plant and two coal plants, the resulting hydro, wind and wood waste projects created twice as many jobs."

Before I go on, there is one criticism that I must pre-empt. It is true that current manufacturing processes for solar panels, wind turbines and other infrastructure for renewable energy require fossil fuels. Fossil fuel lobbyists like to repeat that point until the cows come home. But—as others have pointed out—that apparent contradiction only clarifies the path ahead. The obvious thing to do is this: use fossil fuels already filling existing pipelines strategically, allocating most of them towards building the transition to renewable energy at a global scale.

So what part of "obvious" is not obvious? Why are we push-ing addictive drugs at a rehab centre by even considering more infrastructures for fossil fuel exports?

I guess I know the answer. Neoclassical economics, which dominates the current economic world view, is driven by the in-terests of individuals demanding access to goods, regardless of the environmental and social costs of manufacturing and transporting these goods. Many neoclassical economists have deluded them-selves into thinking that human ingenuity and technology are so amazing that they can overcome any and all environmental prob-lems. Typical of this thinking is Robert Solow, winner of the 1987 Nobel Prize in economics, who famously claimed that "the world can, in effect, get along without natural resources." The tenets of neoclassical economics are so naïve that, in the words of writer Paul Hawken, they "have created an economic system that tells us it is cheaper to destroy the Earth than it is to maintain it."

But the genius who invented walking can do better than that.

When economists with enough temerity to dig their heads out of the sand and see ecosystems for what they really are go through the numbers, a whole new picture emerges. In the world view of ecological economics—a discipline that is actually sane—keeping carbon sequestered in the ground or forests, instead of releasing it into the atmosphere where it unleashes extreme weather, melts the icecaps, and generally robs us of our good times, is worth trillions of dollars in avoided hardship.

If I had a rocket launcher, some son of a bitch would die

I know, I know, I know… To paraphrase Tsleil-Waututh climate defender Rueben George and my long-term activist friends Dan Lewis and Bonny Glambeck, we must act out of love for what we want to protect, not out of hate for those who are wrecking it. Twyla Bella, during a powerful speech that you witnessed with Gail and me, Bernice King, the youngest daugh-ter of Dr. Martin Luther King Jr., reminded us of a profound truth: "Hate will destroy the hater more than the hated." So as much as I may fantasize about putting a rocket launcher to good use, at the end of the day I always land here: love for the

Earth comes first, and from that love springs the motivation to act on the Earth's behalf.

These were my thoughts as you, Gail and I stood in front of the offices of Port Metro Vancouver one chilly February day in 2013, participating in a rally organized by Kids For Climate Action, a group of eloquent teenagers determined to have a say in their own future. These kids knew that 2012 marked the 333rd consecutive month of above-average global temperatures, and that the 6-percent rise in global food prices that occurred during that year was not a coincidence. They knew that they were the ones who will live with the rising costs of food production, the rising frequency of extreme storms like Hurricane Sandy, the rising of sea levels, the changing chemistry of the ocean that already threatens marine life and fisheries, and the social and economic unrest associated with those events.

Their speeches asked the Port for accountability to their generation. The Port has consistently told them, and the rest of us, that climate change is not their problem. They are just fulfilling their mandate: promoting international trade and creating jobs for British Columbia.

Analogs of this business model are clichéd by now. Tobacco companies have generated tremendous economic activity, never mind the destructiveness of their cigarettes to human health. The arms industry generates billions in worldwide weapons sales ($44 billion in 2011 alone), never mind the genocidal regimes and radical militant groups who use those arms.

After the speeches, Rhythm Kids, a performing group of five- to twelve-year-olds that uses rope jumping, dance and rhymes to express their generation's rights to a healthy planet, performed. Gail was the choreographer and you, Twyla Bella, one of the performers.

As I watched you and your friends join our attempts to do something about the climate crisis, I was reminded of what you sensed that day at your very first climate rally, when you were only five: something serious is happening, and that something is not going to go away easily.

Even if society suddenly decided to start cutting emissions

and transitioning towards renewable energies, the way of life that most people take for granted would have to change. Yet there is strong evidence that whole industrialized societies can shift, fundamentally and with good style, once they decide to listen—and I mean really listen—to the data.

SEVEN DECADES AGO, THE most industrialized and car-loving nation in the entire history of humanity showed that it is possible to power down, en masse, and that doing so builds community. In a 2007 essay published in *Sierra* magazine, American writer Mike Davis paints a picture of the United States during World War II unrecognizable today:

> In the 1940s, Americans simultaneously battled fascism overseas and waste at home. My parents, their neighbors, and millions of others left cars at home to ride bikes to work, tore up their front yards to plant cabbage, recycled toothpaste tubes and cooking grease, volunteered at daycare centers and USOs, shared their houses and dinners with strangers, and conscientiously attempted to reduce unnecessary consumption and waste.

Critically, Davis goes on to explain, "The war also temporarily dethroned the automobile as the icon of the American standard of living." Car factories were transformed into assembly lines for tanks and other war machines while rubber for tires and gasoline had to be rationed. This new normal, Davis continues, stigmatized single-person occupancy of a car: "Car sharing was reinforced by gas-ration incentives, stiff fines for solo recreational driving, and stark slogans: 'When you ride ALONE,' warned one poster, 'you ride with Hitler!'" It also brought people together by making hitch-hiking "an officially sanctioned form of ride sharing" to the point that "the Republican Party [in Colorado] vowed to save rubber by having all of its candidates in the 1944 elections hitchhike to campaign rallies."

And dethroning the car made everyone healthier.

> With recreational driving curtailed by rationing, families toured and vacationed by bike. In June 1942, park officials reported that "never has bicycling been so popular in Yosemite Valley as it is this season." Public health officials praised the dual contributions of victory gardening [planting kitchen gardens to cope with wartime food shortages] and bike riding to enhanced civilian vigor and well-being, even predicting that it might reduce the already ominously increasing cancer rate.

After the war, the United States powered back up, squelching the opportunity to maintain a low-carbon economy and the exceptional levels of community spirit and public health that go with it. Yet the capacity of industrialized nations to power down when needed resurfaced during the 1970s OPEC oil embargo. University of Lancaster sociologist John Urry explains:

> Some effects [of the embargo] included switching to smaller European and Japanese cars; significant growth in carpooling and public transport; calls for a tax to subsidize mass transit; a doubling of fuel efficiency of cars; some alternative energy developments such as geothermal, solar and windpower; President Jimmy Carter suggesting keeping homes at lower temperatures; and limits placed upon the use of oil and gas in generating electricity. Elsewhere developments included carfree days especially in New Zealand, government requests in the UK for households to heat only one room [...] and much shifting to natural gas away from coal and oil for electricity generation. Significantly these developments occurred before "digital lives" had become a possible element of a lower carbon future.

Yet this transformation of society did not last. The elections of Ronald Reagan in the United States and Margaret Thatcher in the United Kingdom during the 1980s resurrected neo-liberal capitalism. Although the opportunity to keep treading more gently on the planet was, once again, squandered, the oil embargo did show, once again, that large societies can change quickly and consume less fossil fuels.

John Urry argues that today's rising fuel prices are already creating the preconditions that could give us a third chance, allowing "green shoots of a powering down" to sprout in key places. His analyses show that we are past the peak of globalization, and that some of the world's richest nations are past the "the peaking of stuff and of travel." British residents have been consuming less material goods and burning less fuel since the early to mid-2000s, even as incomes and populations continue to rise. Revealingly, he refers to a survey in the United States in which "46 percent of 18- to 24-year-olds said they would choose Internet access over owning their own car, while the figure is 15 percent for baby boomers." For the nation that invented the twelve-lane freeway and all of its glory, that is a sign of astonishing change.

But as upbeat as that sounds, it is too early to get excited about what might come out of these preconditions. That third chance to transform industrialized societies for real will not happen as long as the fossil fuel industry is allowed to keep lobbying governments and funding the climate change denial industry—effectively buying out democracy—while receiving public subsidies that are many times larger than those received by the renewable energy industries.

TWYLA BELLA, I DO not claim that powering down is easy or convenient. In fact, this is where everyone, including us, has to take a good look at themselves in the mirror. I, for one, would love to show you more of my native country of Mexico, yet the jet-flying quota that our family allocates itself curtails that option until, sometime in the not-so-near future, we can find the time to travel overland. Recently, I lamented that casualty of climate change awareness to my friend Dan Lewis. His response was rather unsympathetic: "It was never a legitimate option. Cheap flights that allow you to reach faraway places, instantly and for non-essential reasons, are the artifact of a society that buries its head in the sand. Not flying when you can avoid it is a gain for Twyla, not a loss of her life experience." Dan, of course, was right, and I knew that already.

The year before, in 2012, I had written an article for *Conservation Bytes* where I asked: "Who is responsible for climate change? Not us ecologists, right?" The piece argued that ecologists should rethink their laissez-faire attitude towards hopping on a jet plane and gallivanting across the globe for conferences, meetings, even fieldwork—multiple times each year—as the typical academic does. By choosing field sites closer to home (at least within the same country) and using video-conferencing, we could still get out in the field and continue to exchange ideas in real time without ripping apart what we are trying to protect through our hypocritical endorsement of the jet industry. (By the way, the article generated all sorts of positive discussion and great ideas, yet most ecologists continue to burn jet fuel like there is no tomorrow, criss-crossing the world in the name of saving it. Go figure.)

My article was inspired by Kevin Anderson, deputy director of the Tyndall Centre for Climate Change Research at the University of Manchester. He is arguably the climate conscience of scientists. Anderson calls air travel "the most emissions-profligate activity per hour." He has little patience for the irony that "international climate jamborees," otherwise known as climate science meetings, have contributed far more to increasing carbon emissions than to any meaningful action on climate change. Even purchasing offsets with a plane ticket lets nobody off the hook. These purchases fund projects in the developing world that capture atmospheric carbon through reforestation or reduce emissions through renewable energy, and many people view them as a legitimate means to fly guilt-free. Not Anderson. Writing in *Nature*, he argues that "offsetting is worse than doing nothing. It is without scientific legitimacy, is dangerously misleading and almost certainly contributes to a net increase in the absolute rate of global emissions growth."

Carbon offsets are flawed, says Anderson, because greenhouse gases remain in the atmosphere for one to ten centuries and offset projects exist within a carbon-driven economy. A legitimate offset project, therefore, must prove that it can remove an amount of greenhouse gases equal to that produced by the airplane flight plus all additional emissions generated by the offset project, both directly and indirectly, for one hundred to a thousand years. "To do so," writes Anderson, "would presume powers of prediction that could have foreseen the Internet and low-cost airlines following from Marconi's 1901 telegraph and the Wright brothers' 1903 maiden flight." His scepticism stems from the tight link between perceived prosperity and fossil fuel consumption espoused by our current economic system. That is, offsetting projects almost invariably boost emissions indirectly in the developing world, by generating cash to be spent on cars or other commodities that consume fossil fuels. Anderson clarifies that he is "not opposed to funding those in poorer communities; but again this has nothing to do with offsetting so why refer to it as such?"

Unafraid to tell it like it is, Anderson quips in his blog:

> Jump on a plane and you send a signal that says please buy some more aircraft that will have a 20–30 year operating life and a design life of typically around 40 years. Please build some more airports; divert your public transport funding to ensure I can travel from the centre of the nearby city to the airport in a low-carbon manner (before leaping on the pinnacle of humankind's carbon-emitting ingenuity); please also expand the car park (these 'always' expand in absolute terms more than the public transport); and please ensure we keep seeking out the black stuff—because without it we will have invested billions on an industry dependent on kerosene—lock-in *par excellence*. They don't tell you all this on the back of the ticket—though there may be some *oh so useful* advice on carbon offsetting—odd again how emissions

aren't coming down when we can buy *indulgences* so easily and cheaply?

Leading by example, Anderson has avoided flying for nearly a decade. In 2011 he took a slow train to Shanghai from the U.K. to open a new research centre, ten days out and eleven days back. When I asked him about the time costs to his busy academic life, he replied that "despite the value of the destination, the journey was the most productive and enjoyable period of my academic career. I wrote a paper on the way out and almost completed another on the return. A slow-moving, perfectly comfortable and pleasantly battered carriage was a conducive environment for thinking and research." Anderson then added that the slowness of overland travel "forces us to travel much less, be much more selective in what we attend and to endeavour to get more out of those trips we do take. Fewer trips and potentially longer stays: not rocket science, just unpalatable climate change basics."

I love the ring of that last phrase: "Unpalatable climate change basics." Every time I say it out loud, the fundamental action that individuals could take to slow down the rate at which the biosphere is plummeting becomes so obvious: Slow down and feel the ground beneath your feet, right where you live.

TWYLA BELLA, NOW THAT you are becoming a big kid and into watching crazy action flicks, you've become familiar with the classic movie formula in which monsters and bad guys never die; they just go dormant for a short time after receiving a good beating from the hero. And then, just as the hero is catching his or her breath, some blob appears from a cloud in the sky and turns into Godzilla, all over again. That's the fossil fuel industry for you.

So on November 22, 2014, I landed in jail again. That day I crossed an injunction line on Burnaby Mountain, near the campus of Simon Fraser University in Greater Vancouver, where Houston-based Kinder Morgan was conducting survey work to expand the Trans Mountain pipeline so that they could bring even more climate-destroying bitumen from the Alberta tar sands to the port of Vancouver for export to Asia.

My arrest was the fifty-third one that week (more than fifty more were still to come). It meant handcuffs, a paddy wagon ride and almost eight hours under custody, including about four hours in solitary confinement in a cold cell without food or water. While the police treated us courteously (as we treated them), I could not help wondering whether the solitary confinement reflected top-down orders from corporate boardrooms.

Was this second act of peaceful civil disobedience consistent with my obligations as a parent, human being and scientist? Absolutely. As a scientist, I know that we've had a very sweet deal for the last twelve thousand years. One hundred and twenty centuries with enough ice caps to regulate our sea levels, just the right amount of Arctic sea ice to guarantee the air circulation patterns that bring good conditions for agriculture, just the right ocean chemistry to allow the many fishes and plankton that support us to thrive…a uniquely friendly stage in Earth's history that allowed civilization to develop. And as a parent and human being, it is just not in my nature to sit back passively and watch the destruction of that sweet deal without trying to do something about it.

Yet, not being one to water down my message, I must also tell you that the sweet climate deal that babied us for so long is now history. More frequent and extreme droughts and storms are already becoming the new global normal. We are onto something much less pretty now, but I would not get too upset about it. I really mean that. The opportunities to steer ourselves towards the path of greater resilience are still here. Which is why people need each other more than ever before.

Twyla Bella, don't let anybody tell you that genius and destroyer must be the same. Humans invented walking to step into something beautiful—an unprecedented rise of creativity, consciousness and wisdom. As you know from our times snuggled up together, reading aloud bedtime stories about the Universe, we are stardust, literally. Carbon, oxygen and other elements essential to most life on Earth originated inside stars that exploded into supernovas, and spread across space until they become us. I like to think that our origins gave us the capacity to shine, endlessly.

In a less combative moment, Kevin Anderson wrote with his colleague, Alice Bows, "The world is moving on and we need to have the audacity to think differently and conceive of alternative futures."

I know we can do this.

Love,
Pops

CHAPTER 7

Irrevocable Change

Dear Twyla Bella,

I walk through the forest experiencing parallel universes. In a way, I am very much here. Aware of twigs on the ground that I do not wish to crunch, noisily, with body weight transferred by feet. Breathing the frosty air, slowly, deeply. Observing the twilight illuminate spaces between trees and swordferns where deer, my quarry, might stand.

Yet I am also far away, lost in thoughts about the Anthropocene—this current era of Earth's history in which human consumption drives most biophysical processes. I walk in a bit of a stupor, stunned by the fact that, in the mere blink of the eye since the industrial revolution, we have altered the fate of water, land and atmosphere for millennia to come. Global temperatures have increased by 0.8 degrees Celsius in the last century. This is old news. Yet I was recently shocked into a new level of understanding when, studying a graph by James Hansen and colleagues, I realized that three-quarters of that temperature rise occurred since the mid-1970s. I was born in 1964. To paraphrase writer and climate activist Bill McKibben, this is, literally, not the same planet I was born in.

My parallel universes have a confluence. This hunt is one of my peace treaties. With myself or some other entity, I am not sure. A peace treaty, nonetheless.

Earlier this morning I kayaked to this island in pre-dawn

winter darkness. At the start of the paddle, the channel seemed wild and remote, although Howe Sound is anything but that. After I rounded a corner, the glow of Vancouver's city lights appeared on the horizon. As always, I had to dodge the monstrous commuter ferry that travels back and forth across these waters. And my awareness that old-growth forests are no more, that settlers killed the last wolf pack of these islands nearly a hundred years ago, would not shut up.

A peace treaty, nonetheless.

In case you are wondering what this "peace treaty" stuff is all about, I better explain. Up until now, my letters have relied on science to give you a sense of the challenges facing the biosphere today, and the fundamental changes that society is perfectly capable of undertaking—right now—to deal with these challenges. But science is only a compass. That's it. On its own, it cannot be the kick in the butt that propels us in any given direction. That is why we need stories that might help us make sense of where we are and where we might go. As the great native writer Thomas King wrote in his 2003 Massey Lectures book, "The truth about stories is that that's all we are." And the stories I tell myself today are ones that might help me find peace in the Anthropocene.

Soon after I landed on this island, I became keenly aware of how my feet connect with the ground. Large big-leaf maples and red cedars near the edge of the sea had made a corridor for my stalking of deer. Walking among those trees, I thought of how native people getting back on their feet after residential schools already live the sorts of resilience we will need to make our way through the Anthropocene. This is not some abstract concept for you, Twyla Bella. You have lived it by spending time with indigenous people who, like Earth itself, have changed irrevocably under colonialism and industrialization. Yet their essence endures.

IN 2010, WHEN YOU were six, you stood on a river gravel bar on a late October day. A few orange leaves still clung to deciduous trees. Dressed in red pants, light blue jacket, purple hat and yellow life jacket, you stood out, not only because of your colourful outfit but because you were the only kid in a pack of indigenous people, biologists and activists. We were spending the week paddling down the lower Fraser River—one of North America's most important wild salmon rivers—into Vancouver Harbour. The event was drawing public attention to scientific evidence suggesting that disease and parasites emanating from open-net salmon farms were harming wild salmon.

Among people from the Stó:lō, Squamish, Musqueam, Tsleil-Waututh, Xeni Gwet'in and other nations whose ancestry is deeply rooted in this river and its tributaries, we had been participating in nightly salmon celebrations full of song and fire. You had spoken at sharing circles and been honoured with songs from native elders. Yet for me, the remarkable thing was that the urban infrastructure of Greater Vancouver had surrounded us for most of the journey. And somehow, the gritty pavement and traffic noise had only deepened the experience.

The gravel bar where you stood was no exception. The concrete, steel and roaring traffic of a massive highway bridge towered above. I was tempted to see the bridge and highway as monsters that had chomped off the rich wetlands that once existed here. It was then that Gilbert Salomon, a spiritual leader of the Xeni Gwet'in nation, walked near you and began to beat his drum, singing in Tsilhqot'in with a voice that transcended all languages and visible worlds. As Gilbert sang, the surrounding urban junk vanished from my reality. I could see only the water that touched your rubber boots—the same medium through which millions of sockeye, spring, coho and chum salmon had just swum on their way to spawning grounds thousands of kilometres upstream.

Throughout our downriver journey, wherever we switched from one First Nation territory to another or sought to go ashore, representatives of the local nation would be anticipating our arrival. In our canoes we would hold our paddle blades upwards, showing respect while exchanges in Coast Salish languages would communicate the ancestry of the speakers, the goal of our journey and the request and granting of permission to proceed.

Listening to these formal expressions of lineage and diplomacy in traditional languages, I could feel why this urbanized river remained the very spirit of our hosts and travelling companions. We were witnessing the endurance of living cultures that are still nourished by wild salmon, no matter the sprawling suburbs and shopping malls.

Months later, I visited Gilbert at his home by Chilko Lake, at the eastern edge of the Coast Mountains of southwestern British Columbia. Unlike First Nations whose territories lie within Greater Vancouver, Gilbert's people live in one of the province's least developed, wildest territories—far from urban centres, mountainous, still full of grizzly bears and other carnivores. This has not happened out of blind luck, but rather out of a fighting spirit— one in favour of salmon, trout and traditional culture—that has been applied against invaders since at least 1864. That year, Gilbert's ancestors repelled from their territory a road-building crew working for Alfred Waddington, a colonial entrepreneur. Ever since, anybody wanting to mine or log in Xeni Gwet'in territory encounters articulate and fierce opposition.

Over the course of a few days, Gilbert and I watched squalls swallow mountains and sweep across the turquoise waters. We came upon bear sign as we picked b'iek—saskatoon berries—with his granddaughters. We told stories from our lives.

Despite their fierce spirit and the remoteness of their territory, the Xeni Gwet'in were not spared Canada's institutionalized racism. Gilbert, too, like the lost wetlands of the lower Fraser River, was imprisoned as a child under the weight of concrete, steel and bars—one hundred months at residential schools, where he was taken from his family and forbidden to speak his language. To give me a sense of the damage, Gilbert recalled the summer when he was six. At the start of that season, upon being released for two months from residential school, he rode home with his older brothers on a horse wagon. When they reached their family's seasonal camp, Gilbert asked, "Who is that woman working over there?" At first, his brothers did not know what to say, but eventually they had to respond. After spending most of his early childhood in residential school, Gilbert had failed to recognize his own mother.

Of course the experience had broken him, but not permanently. As an adult, drawing from songs and stories in his language, he had rebounded into something like the Fraser River water that salmon travel through under a suburban highway bridge. Gilbert had become a conduit for the spiritual nourishment of his people, helping the Xeni Gwet'in navigate through the thick of the Anthropocene, without losing sight of their source.

A COUPLE OF YEARS later in Haida Gwaii, Twyla Bella, your experience of language and resilience grew. You were eight when we joined a canoe journey to the southern part of the archipelago. It was then that we got to know Captain Gold, a Haida elder and one of the original forces behind the Windy Bay blockades of 1985, which led to the designation and protection of Gwaii Haanas National Park Reserve and Haida Heritage Site, which we were travelling through.

One day you sat near Captain Gold as he used his oversized paddle as a rudder, prying it vertically to steer the massive canoe through thick fog while a dozen paddlers powered forward. With no GPS or compass on hand, he navigated a maze of small rocky islands. The occasional thinning of fog revealed ripples created by black rockfish as they neared the surface, feeding on small fish amidst the upper kelp canopy. Pigeon guillemots, marbled murrelets and other seabirds flashed in and out of the mist. We travelled off the eastern shore of Lyell Island on a replica of *Lootaas*, a fifteen-metre-long cedar canoe built with traditional techniques by Haida artists in the 1980s. This area was familiar to you; this was the fourth year in a row that I had come here to participate in studies of rocky reef ecology, and you had joined me for the last two seasons.

With fieldwork now over, it was time for you and Gail and I to immerse ourselves in this canoe journey. And I was feeling pretty good that, inside the fog, I could narrow down our location to within a kilometre or so. But I also knew that my spatial awareness was inferior to whatever traditional techniques Captain Gold was invoking. A few hours later, the fog still thick, the canoe landed *precisely* on the small island we had aimed for. Whether Captain Gold had taken cues from the direction of the breeze, the rebound patterns of waves against the rocks or the strength and direction of the tide, I will never know. He did not offer to tell and this was not the sort of knowledge I could casually ask about.

Captain Gold had taken a liking to you, the one young child among towering adults and teenagers. Impressed by your assertiveness, he nicknamed you The Boss. When we visited Hotsprings Island, Kathleen (Golie) Hans—the matriarch of her clan, the Naa 'Yuu'ans Skidegate Gidins, whose proud Haida name is SG̲aana Jaads K'yaga X̲iigangs—turned that nickname into a proper Haida name, Nang K'uulas, which translates as "Boss Woman." Golie made sure we understood that this was not some casual fancy: only elders of her status could gift someone a Haida name. And her fluency in the Haida language was the poetry of resilience. Most members of Golie's generation had been forced to "forget" their language, beaten for speaking it in government residential schools. Yet somehow Golie had escaped those horrors as a child. And today, thanks to her and other elders, schoolchildren on the islands are being taught the Haida language.

As the journey went on, the words "change," "resilience" and "adaptation" dominated my thoughts. After all, our replica of *Lootaas* was cast in an archetypically modern material: fibreglass. And Robert Vogstad, a fellow paddler whose Haida name is Luptaagaa, was fast becoming a family friend.

Luptaagaa is a neo-traditional artist firmly rooted in his twelve thousand years of ancestry in these islands—and schooled in modern art. His carvings on argillite or cedar and his paintings build on traditional designs, yet also draw from the melting pot of ideas and cultures he has experienced while studying in cities. After the canoe journey, while we toured his studio, his painting of a salmon shark hunting salmon immediately grabbed me. Everything about it felt familiar, like a fibreglass version of *Lootaas* steered by Captain Gold. I had seen salmon sharks slice calm surface waters with their dorsal fins in Prince William Sound, Alaska. But beyond that glimpse in the wild, I knew them as top predators predicted to experience severe range contractions as a result of climate change. Of course we bought the painting.

Ever since, I begin my winter mornings in pre-dawn darkness, lighting the wood stove and candle so that I may enter the day by stretching my muscles and filling my lungs with deep breaths. On each of these mornings comes a moment when I turn during an asana and, bathed in firelight, my gaze lands on Luptaagaa's painting.

Twyla Bella, we all want something that holds things together. Some form of connection to our past, some sort of guidance for uncertain futures. Over the course of hundreds of mornings, Luptaagaa's painting has become such a thing for me. In it, he drew human forms—possibly representing ancestors—nested within prey, the salmon. He also drew his self-portrait on the fin of the top predator, the salmon shark.

My interpretation—and I have never discussed this with him—is that in doing so he acknowledged that while all humans are inseparable from the natural world, each individual has personal connections and responsibilities towards that larger cycle of life. But perhaps most importantly, the painting depicts the best we might do in the face of irrevocable change: embrace it without losing our essence.

Created with modern materials and techniques, the painting is a novel art form that did not exist before European colonization and that emerged from the synergies of modern and Haida cultures. Clearly, colonization has not been all good; the legacies of industrial logging and residential schools are obvious examples of that. Yet within all that bad stuff, artists like Luptaagaa, who are not short of a sense of humour, are the ultimate symbols of resilience. And resilience, not conservation, is the key word.

Twyla Bella, think of conservation as trying to put on the brakes before going off the cliff. Think of resilience as the ability to use a parachute and control your landing after you are thrown off a cliff.

What I think artists like Luptaagaa tell us when they place themselves within the fin of a salmon shark, is that we can still act in a good way. Not by trying to stop ecosystem changes—which at this stage would be entirely futile—but by steering those changes towards the path of greatest resilience. The indigenous people we personally know are already doing it. Perhaps that is a model for what is possible at a much greater scale.

MY DEER HUNT GOES on without much happening, at least outside my mind. Wishing to reset my headspace, I begin to heighten my external senses by whispering, internally, the words "gratitude," "intention" and "focus," repeatedly, in sync with each slow step I take.

Until I dip my hands into the steaming, open cavity of a deer.

My intellectual self is quick to remind me that my hunting success is an artifact. The extirpation of wolves by those fearful settlers one hundred years ago, no doubt, has made my hunt easier than it would have been had top predators still been here. My saner self counters: "what-friggin-ever…the deal is sealed so I may as well enjoy it," imagining that Luptaagaa might laugh at my little conversation. In any case, this is not about easier hunting, but rather about adapting to irrevocable change. Wolves never will be reintroduced to the islands of Howe Sound and—given our limited resources to deal with the broader climate and biodiversity crises—it would be misguided to do so.

I had shot the deer through the head and its eyes had clouded over by the time I reached its inert body. So I am a bit surprised when I cut through the diaphragm and find the heart still beating for another half minute or so.

Back by the kayak, I hang the deer from a large cedar branch and skin it. When I saw off the hooves I look into rich, pinkish marrow inside the shank bones. This is the very raw material that early hominids learned to suck from crushed ungulate bones, gaining the nutrients that allowed the human brain to evolve towards a larger size and greater creativity.

As I kayak towards home and into the dimming twilight, headless deer stowed inside my back hatch, I think of how the world in which you will breathe your last breath (and may that breath come many—and I mean *many*—decades into the future) will be vastly different from the one in which you exhaled your first cry as a newborn. Twyla Bella, coming to terms with that reality has been the most difficult challenge I have faced as a father. At the same time, the synergy of science and stories that shapes my life has led me to believe that, once we acknowledge the fundamental reality of the Anthropocene and make our peace with that reality, the genius who invented walking will commit him- and herself towards the path of greater resilience.

My paddle blades ignite sparkles of bioluminescence each time they touch the water. I am enjoying myself immensely until that damn ferry heading my way jolts me back into the Anthropocene. So I rise to the adrenalized occasion, pumping faster strokes. Once out of harm's way, I stop paddling to catch my breath. The kayak keeps gliding, leaving behind a bioluminescent trail. An overwhelming love for Earth—no matter the irrevocable changes—swells within me.

Within a couple hours we will slice and eat that deer heart in celebration while marrow soup cooks on the wood stove. The wolves may be gone, but our ancestral food is still here.

Love,
Pops

A Birth Story

Dear Twyla Bella,

Resilience in the Anthropocene is entirely possible, but far from a done deal. For it to happen at all, our collective actions will have to propagate at a large scale, steering us towards a lower-carbon and less-consumptive way of life, sooner than later. This has yet to happen. So we stand on tenuous ground that will continue to hold, but not for long.

The precarious position of humanity reminds me of an experience I once had with a dying skiff engine off the coast of Alaska during a February storm. A skiff engine that belches smoke and then decides to keel over can have vastly different implications, depending on its timing. If it runs just long enough to reach shelter, then you can glide smoothly, regroup with the scattered parts of yourself and celebrate. If it dies half a minute too soon, you are in for a nasty drift into the rocks, chaos and an uncertain future. That dying skiff engine also happens to colour the story of your birth.

The day you were born—three and half weeks before expected—I was on the deck of the commercial fishing vessel *Alexandra*, near Applegate Rocks in a remote part of Prince William Sound, Alaska. All of my attention focused on tracking harbour seals we had equipped with transmitters that emitted radio signals I could receive and follow, and pressure sensors that recorded the depths and durations of their dives. This was part of the ecological research for my dissertation. Things were going well. A stretch of clear, calm weather had allowed me and the team I worked with to track seals and study the fish schools on which they feed non-stop for several days and nights. Stillness had come with cold temperatures, freezing small bays and challenging our ability to find anchorages. But the weather had shifted that day, becoming milder and much stormier.

In the late morning, a radio call from the coast guard told me that Gail was in labour. I knew right away that I would not make it to the birth. In fact I hoped I wouldn't, wishing Gail's labour to be much shorter than the long trip home. But how should I head home? Poor visibility made a floatplane pickup impossible. The only option was to board the Boston whaler with one of my colleagues, Jay Ver Hoef, and go for a ninety-mile ride to the community of Whittier, facing the prospect of snow squalls, strong winds and high chop. Expertly piloted by Jay, the skiff should have been able to manage all that—assuming its 150-horsepower engine kept working.

As it turned out, the engine's remaining health was timed perfectly to take us beyond radio contact with the *Alexandra* and close to nowhere. While crossing to Perry Island during a particularly snowy and windy part of the storm, the power dropped and we slowed to a desperate crawl. Uncertainty turned everything into eternal slow motion, and—since I do not believe in suffering twice—I breathed deeply to stave off images of a dead engine and a long drift into a crash landing. Somehow, we chugged along through the crossing, found a calm spot, fiddled around with apparently loose connections (a standard placebo for incompetent mechanics), and motored on with what seemed to be a resuscitated engine.

Well's Passage, the next big crossing, was raucous and an even worse place for an engine to fail. Large waves crashed on steep cliffs downwind from us. Our thoughts willed the engine to just keep performing, at least long enough to make the other side.

It was around then that Gail breathed you into the world.

The moment we reached the other side of Well's Passage and entered the calm waters of a narrow fjord, the engine died beyond resuscitation. (In retrospect, we may have had a freezing carburetor that could have been warmed up, but we failed to consider that at the time.) Heavy snowfall muffled all sounds, accentuating the sudden silence. Common murres glided just above the water, disappearing into ethereal mist, emerging out of snowflakes. We had entered the edge of radio contact with Whittier. Within hours we were towed into harbour. Roads and airplanes swept me through the night (the fossil-fuel-burning hypocrisy does not escape me), and I reached you and Gail seventeen hours after you were born.

Years later, I now see society's potential response to the climate change crisis as a skiff engine about to die during a winter storm. And so I am back in Well's Passage, breathing deeply to not suffer twice, filled with a sense of possibility for the reshaping of the modern psyche and economy into a system that values ecosystems and intergenerational justice. That system would provide the tools and motivation to wean society from fossil fuels and reduce greenhouse gases to a level at which people can continue to live safely, coexisting with our remaining non-human kin. Yet that reshaping of human awareness and responsibility to the biosphere will succeed only if the speed of our response matches the imminence of the potential disaster. An atmospheric CO_2 level that commits us to the disintegration of the polar ice caps and runaway climate change is not far away and only looming closer.

A skiff engine can die seconds short of its mark and create a huge mess. A skiff engine can die after entering safety, allowing for better possibilities.

Prince William Sound during February squalls. Well's Passage and its aftermath. I have this image that, at the very moment of your emergence, the energy that poured out of Gail's birth canal and into the world is what kept the skiff engine going for those extra seconds that got us into shelter. I may have not been at the birth, yet the birth was there with me.

Love,
Pops

Afterword

A year and half has gone by since I first completed this manuscript, and much has happened since. Highlights include spending time with Twyla Bella (now eleven years old) and Gail climbing Douglas firs with rope systems (an activity inspired by a book on canopy research the three of us read aloud), snorkelling local reefs and blasting on skis through fresh powder snow. My work with Central Coast First Nations—my connection with the people and seascape—has only intensified. I am particularly fond of the field trips in which Twyla Bella has proven to be an able assistant: controlling the towed video camera we use to survey deep-water habitats or getting her hands covered in fish slime while opening rockfish skulls to extract otoliths (the ear bones we use to age fish). All of this time, my field journals have kept gathering notes that I hope to put to use some day: tales about long-lining for halibut and rockfish with a hereditary chief, humpback whales feeding on spawning herring, my efforts to help First Nations (and the rest of us) navigate a rapidly changing ocean under escalating concentrations of atmospheric CO_2.

While my manuscript sat in unpublished limbo, I had plenty of time to reflect back on the original question that prompted the writing: "What kind of world will be handed down to my daughter's generation?"

Like all really important questions, I knew from the outset that this one was not about to be answered easily, if at all. In writing the book, I had embarked on a path that might at least bring me closer to an answer, a search for genuine optimism amidst the climate change and biodiversity crises. All along, I knew that it would be futile to look for a Hollywood-style happy ending, where—after the angst and struggle are done—we all sit at the beach sipping margaritas and congratulate ourselves about how cool it was to have knocked off the asteroid from its course, in the nick of time before it obliterated Earth.

Instead, I had gone in search of something a lot more nuanced: a world view that recognized the irrevocable changes industrialized society has thrust upon our planet, while still envisioning a way of steering our path towards a place of greater resilience.

As in all journeys of significance, I found something that I did not even know I was looking for: a way to look at my daughter and imagine her many possible futures.

Alejandro Frid
June 27, 2015

Acknowledgements

My deepest, heartfelt gratitude...

To Audrey Grescoe and Paul Grescoe, who volunteered as my main editors and advisors on this project. My debt to them is huge.

To James Mackinnon, Pete Willis, Lynne Quarmby, Chris Darimont and Daniel Wood, who commented on early versions of the manuscript; their encouragement and advice sealed my commitment to completing the work. I also thank Corey Bradshaw, who allowed me to use *Conservation Bytes* to test ideas that were professionally risky, and Lois Moorcroft, whose critical insights improved Chapter 5.

To Sage Birchwater, who introduced me to Caitlin Press, and to Vici Johnstone (publisher) and Scott Steedman (editor), who helped me refine the final version.

To my parents, Samuel Frid (1935–2010) and Esther Frid, and Gail's parents, Gerry Lotenberg and Selma Lotenberg, who shaped this book in so many ways.

To my sister, Dianna Frid, whose creativity has always inspired me, and to my brother, Leonardo Frid, who shared the Patagonian channels and continues to share sea, snow and ecological discussions.

To the activists, scientists, naturalists, artists and economists who continue to inspire me, particularly those who shared experiences described in this book, and to my myriad mentors over the decades, both inside and outside university halls.

To the indigenous people I work with or simply know, who keep teaching me what it means to be deeply rooted, living in interrelationship with our non-human kin. I have been incredibly lucky to have formed relationships with many individuals from many First Nations, including Carcross/Tagish, Haida, Xeni Gwet'in, Kitasoo/Xai'Xais, Wuikinuxv, Heiltsuk, Nuxalk and others. These individuals are too numerous to name here, but suffice it to say that they have gifted me with some of the most powerful lessons of my life. They have jolted me into feeling institutionalized racism in my gut, rather than just understanding it in my brain; shown me caribou and fish through the lens of subsistence hunters and fishers and—most importantly—inspired me to imagine an alternative vision for the Anthropocene, one in which the essence of humanity endures in this "tough new planet" (as Bill McKibben refers to Earth these days).

And of course, to Gail Lotenberg and Twyla Bella Frid Lotenberg, for the dancing, optimism and love.

NOTES

This book uses science and storytelling to make a point. It is not a comprehensive review of the challenges and potential solutions that currently affect the biosphere. The topics I cover reflect my personal experience as a scientist, parent and human being, and the most salient aspects of my awareness at the time of writing.

On a more technical matter, throughout the book I refer to carbon dioxide (CO_2), which is the most abundant and longest-lived greenhouse gas. Yet there are other greenhouse gases, including methane, nitrous oxide, ozone and dimethylsulphide. Greenhouse gas emissions, therefore, sometimes are discussed in terms of carbon dioxide *equivalents* (CO_{2e}). These units represent the heat trapped by non-CO_2 greenhouse gases converted to the amount of CO_2 that would cause the same amount of warming. Measures of CO_{2e} sometimes express the sum of CO_2 and other greenhouse gases. Importantly, carbon (which I do not use as a unit in this book) is not the same as CO_2. Rather, one tonne of carbon equals 3.67 tonnes of CO_2 equivalent. All dollar figures are in US currency. Website links listed below were last accessed on June 22, 2015.

INTRODUCTION
Marliave et al. (2009) describe research on the bioherms of Howe Sound. To learn more about these biological communities, see articles in the blog of the Vancouver Aquarium (aquablog.ca/2014/08/glass-castles-on-the-seabed/) and the *Vancouver Sun* (vancouversun.com/touch/story.html?id=11113107).

1. STORMS AND STILLNESS

The short history of climate is drawn primarily from Hansen (2009) and Tripati et al. (2009). Many sources document the anti-science and pro–fossil fuel stance of Stephen Harper's Conservative Government of Canada; for an entry point into these topics, see Turner (2013).

The potential contributions to global warming of different fuels were estimated by Swart & Weaver (2012). My statement that Swart and Weaver's calculations excluded emissions from tar sands production, which are greater than for conventional fossil fuels, and thus underestimate total tar sand emissions by about 17 percent, paraphrases an email communication to me from Neil Swart.

Charpentier et al. (2009) analyze greenhouse gases produced during tar sands extraction. Studies documenting how the melting of Arctic tundra releases greenhouse gases include Oechel et al. (1993). Research on how the loss of reflective sea ice is changing the energy budget of the Arctic include Riihela et al. (2013). Rooney et al. (2012) estimate the loss of carbon sequestration when tar sands destroy peatlands, concluding, "Landscape changes caused by currently approved mines will release between 11.4 and 47.3 million metric tons of stored carbon and will reduce carbon sequestration potential by 5,734–7,241 metric tons [per year]." These authors also point out that plans for land reclamation will fail to restore the land's capacity to store carbon. Nikiforuk (2010) describes the history and current issues of the tar sands.

The speech in which Environment Minister Peter Kent presents himself at the service of industry and mocks the Kyoto protocol is posted at the Environment Canada website: ec.gc.ca/default. asp?lang=En&n=6F2DE1CA-1&news=E3CF6B4F-57F5-4058-A7D8-A1B543584475.

2. VANISHING GLIMPSES

The words of Lakutaia Le Kipa, the last pure-blooded member of the Yagán race, are quoted (with my translation) from Stambuk (1986). My scientific findings on huemul are documented in Frid

(1994, 1999, 2001); these papers cite other studies on the forests and wildlife of southern Chile. Studies on Sitka black-tailed deer and temperate forests of Chile and Alaska that provided a foundation for my huemul research include Schoen and Kirchhoff (1990) and Alaback (1982, 1991). For data suggesting huemul at my former study site have been increasing since cattle removal, see Briceño et al. (2013).

3. Vibrant Tension

The King's Stilts by Dr. Seuss might be best known for its insights into the balance between playing hard and working hard. As far as I know, the ecological interactions depicted in that story had not been acknowledged previously.

Lima and Dill (1990) wrote the classic synthesis on the costs and benefits of antipredator behaviour. Studies on how predation risk from predatory spiders indirectly affects plant communities and ecosystem function include Schmitz (2008); this work provides a template for predicting how large ecosystems might change as big and fierce predators, like sharks and wolves, vanish. Syntheses on the ecological costs of predator declines include Heithaus et al. (2008) and Prugh et al. (2009).

My description of traditional resource use by native cultures of coastal British Columbia is drawn primarily from Turner (1998).

Syntheses on how overfishing alters marine ecosystems include Pauly et al. (2002). Tyedmers et al. (2005) analyze the fuel consumption of industrial fishing fleets. Morato et al. (2006) analyze how fisheries have been depleting progressively deeper depths. Analyses of the impacts of open-net salmon aquaculture on wild salmon include Connors et al. (2012) and Miller et al. (2014). Rowan Trebilco's research on the size-based ecology of predatory fishes is reported in Trebilco et al. (2013) and Trebilco (2014).

The history of sea otter exploitation, reintroduction programs, and human–sea otter competition for shared resources (including contemporary issues) is summarized in the book *Sea Otters of Haida Gwaii* (Sloan & Dick 2012). Jim Estes has spent about four decades pioneering studies on how sea otters influence kelp forest productivity and biodiversity (e.g. Estes et al. 2010). Jane Watson conducted the research on the behavioural responses by urchins to sea otter predation risk (Watson & Estes 2011). Wilmers et al. (2012) analyze the indirect effect of sea otters on sequestration of atmospheric carbon (via kelp forest productivity). Lynn Lee is currently writing up her work on northern abalone and kelp forests along a gradient of sea otter densities.

Todd Golumbia reviews the history of exotic species introductions to the terrestrial habitats of Haida Gwaii (Golumbia 2000). Jean-Louis Martin and colleagues have created a large body of work on the ecological impacts of deer overabundance in Haida Gwaii (e.g. Martin et al. 2010). His former graduate student Gwenaël Vourc'h provided evidence that the original population of red cedar on Haida Gwaii had, on average, a lower concentration of chemical defences against herbivores than on the mainland, and that trees with lower levels of these chemicals were browsed preferentially by deer (e.g. Vourc'h et al. 2001).

My studies of lingcod, rockfish and kelp greenling can be found in the refereed literature (Frid & Marliave 2010; Frid et al. 2012; Frid et al. 2013).

Studies of how ocean acidification may be altering antipredator behaviour of some prey and the hunting abilities of some predators include Ferrari et al. (2011) and Rosa and Seibel (2008). Predictions on how top predators may redistribute themselves in a warming ocean include those modeled by Hazen et al. (2013). Higdon et al. (2012) and other studies document killer whale expansion into the increasingly ice-free Arctic. Cheung et al. (2013) analyze the shrinking body sizes of fish in response to warming temperatures and lower oxygen concentrations in the ocean.

4. CLIMATE AND WAR

Events in the life of photographer W. Eugene Smith are drawn from his biography by Hughes (1999). His photographs of the war in the Pacific and *The Walk To Paradise Garden* can be viewed online at: magnumphotos.com/C.aspx?VP3=SearchResult&ALID=2TY-RYDIJPUY3.

Mirza (2012) and Hauger (2012) presented the talks that I attended at the meeting of the American Association for the Advancement of Science on the security implications of climate change impacts on Bangladesh. At the same meeting, James Hansen—who led the NASA Goddard Institute for Space Studies between 1981 and 2013 and currently is an adjunct professor at Columbia University—provided evidence that extreme weather anomalies occurred ten times more frequently between 1980 and 2010 than during the preceding thirty years (Hansen et al. 2012). Coumou and Rahmstorf (2012) review further evidence that climate change has led to more frequent droughts and extreme storms. The published data on this topic keeps growing and growing; Hansen et al. (2013) provide a recent synthesis. The population density of Bangladesh (1048.3 people per square kilometre in 2012) is as reported by UN data at data.un.org/CountryProfile. aspx?crName=Bangladesh#Summary.

Pioneer studies on dynamic state variable models of animal behaviour include Mangel and Clark (1988). (I had the privilege of having Marc Mangel as the external examiner for my dissertation defence.) The tadpole and wildebeest studies providing early evidence of increased risk-taking by prey under resource scarcity were conducted, respectively, by Anholt and Werner (1995) and Sinclair and Arcese (1995). Our study on the effect of body condition on the behaviour of green turtles at risk of predation by tiger sharks is reported in Heithaus et al. (2007). For a synthesis of research in predator-prey behavioural interactions in Shark Bay, see Heithaus et al. (2012). Mike Heithaus's website introduces the green turtle project and many other studies conducted in Shark Bay: fiu.edu/~heithaus/SBERP/.

For examples of my mathematical models predicting fishery effects on behavioural interactions between pinnipeds and their potential predators, and of my Dall's sheep studies, see, respectively, Frid et al. (2009) and Frid (1997). My research website provides many other examples: alejandrofridecology.weebly.com.

The relationship between climate change, sea-ice loss and human-inflicted mortality of polar bears is documented in Stirling and Parkinson (2006). Zhang et al. (2007) analyzed the relationship between resource scarcity and greater war frequency during the Little Ice Age. Hsiang et al. (2011) analyzed relationships between El Niño Southern Oscillation, drought and increased rates of armed conflicts in tropical countries. I first discussed how these studies relate to predictions from dynamic state variable models in Frid and Heithaus (2010). Books on the relationship between climate change and war include Dyer (2008) and Parenti (2011). Chris Huhne is quoted from Jones (2011a).

My period of obsession with genocide literature began upon reading *Power* (2002). André and Platteau (1998) are the economists whom I quote and who studied how land degradation exacerbated the socioeconomic and political forces that unleashed the Rwandan genocide. The quote by James Orbinski is taken from his haunting book, *An Imperfect Offering* (Orbinski 2008). Giles Peres's shocking images of the Rwandan genocide can be viewed online at magnumphotos.com/C.aspx?VP3=Search Result&ALID=2K7O3RBHGCSE. The mid-nineteenth-century raid among Yukon aboriginal people that I referred to occurred when the White River People decimated their neighbours at Dezadeash Lake (Cruikshank 2005). For an evolutionary perspective on evil, see Watson (1995).

5. WILD FOOD

This chapter is partly inspired by Hugh Brody's book *The Other Side of Eden*. The article in the *Economist* I quote from can be viewed at economist.com/node/1239301. Robert Semeniuk is quoted from his heart-wrenching photo essay "The San: Aids and Dislocation," which can be viewed at robertsemeniuk.com/reportage.html?gallery=12. To learn about the history of residential schools, see the website of the Truth and Reconciliation Commission of Canada: trc.ca/websites/trcinstitution/index.php?p=3.

Yannic et al. (2014) predict changes to caribou distributions in response to climate change; I recommend viewing their Supplementary Figure 6.

References related to the section on the Central Coast of British Columbia include:

- Central Coast Indigenous Alliance: ccira.ca
- Temperate rainforest characteristics: Alaback (1991)
- Climate change and salmon: Taylor (2008) and Miller et al. (2014)
- Salmon-forest relationships, including those mediated by bears: Drake and Naiman (2007) and Quinn et al. (2009)
- Eulachon: Moody and Pitcher (2010), Schweigert et al. (2012) and http://www.nuxalk.net/html/eulachon.htm.
- The importance of maintaining old-age structure in rock-fish and lingcod populations: Berkeley et al. (2004)
- Climate change and fisheries: Doney et al. (2012)

For a sense of Gail's depth and breadth as a dance artist expressing complex issues, see the *Nature* article describing her work with ecologists, Jones (2011b).

6. EVER TRY TO DE-ACIDIFY AN OCEAN?

Pioneer ecologist E.O. Wilson is quoted from a letter he wrote to the Society of Environmental Journalists; see sej.org/support-sej. Drew Dellinger's poem "Hieroglyphic Stairway" appears in his book, *Love Letter to the Milky Way* (Dellinger 2011). For a detailed account of Harper's war against Canadian science and its underlying motivations, see Turner (2013). Hutchings and Post (2013) analyze how gutting Canada's Fisheries Act threatens endangered species.

Studies on the sensitivity of different species of marine larvae to ocean acidification include Wittmann and Portner (2013). Kawaguchi et al. (2013) analyze the fate of Antarctic krill under ocean acidification. Six et al. (2013) provide evidence that ocean acidification can exacerbate global warming, via the release of dimethylsulphide. Jack A. Gilbert is quoted from his commentary in *Nature Climate Change*, where he summarizes research on phytoplankton and ocean warming by Toseland et al. (2013). For a synthesis of climate change impacts in the ocean, see Doney et al. (2012).

Ronald J. Stouffer is quoted from his article in *Nature Climate Change* (Stouffer 2012), where he summarizes research describing why the fossil fuels we emit today can contribute to global warming for the next thousand years, including Solomon et al. (2009). Matthews and Solomon (2013) explain why, despite those well-accepted facts, climate disasters would still be averted if we were to cut emissions sooner than later. The current cost of removing CO_2 from the atmosphere and capturing it underground is as reported by Hansen and colleagues in a public summary of one of their papers (Hansen et al. 2013) (see columbia.edu/~jeh1/mailings/2013/20131202_PopularSciencePlosOneE.pdf). These authors report costs per unit of carbon, which I converted to costs per unit of CO_2 based on a CO_2 to carbon ratio of 3.67.

Sources for my letter to the Smithsonian Conservation Biology Institute include:

- Capacity of the Pacific Trails Pipeline (1 billion cubic feet per day, or 1,000 MMcf/d): This fact was taken from the Pacific Trails Pipeline website in 2012. Since then, the corporate landscape has changed; the original website no longer exists and the latest reincarnation of the project is Kitimat LNG.
- Carbon dioxide equivalency of natural gas (54.4 kg of CO_2 per 1,000 cubic feet of natural gas): US Energy Information Administration eia.gov/environment/emissions/co2_vol_mass.cfm.
- Global annual rate of greenhouse gas emissions in 2012 (52 billion metric tonnes of carbon dioxide equivalent per year, or 52 GtCO2e yr-1): Climatologist Joeri Rogelj as interviewed by Stephen Leahy (see ipsnews.net/2012/12/at-the-edge-of-the-carbon-cliff/). In that interview, Rogelj updates values from Montzka et al. (2011), who estimated the 2009 rate of global emissions at 50 GtCO2e yr-1.
- Concentration of atmospheric carbon dioxide (nearly 400 parts per million) and its annual growth rate (2 parts per million) in May 2013: US National Oceanic and Atmospheric Administration, as posted in co2now.org/. As of May 2015, the concentration is 403.7 parts per million. (Ouch!)

- Upper safe limit of atmospheric carbon dioxide (350 parts per million): Hansen et al. (2013).

Stephen Leahy's article on fugitive emissions from the natural gas industry in British Columbia appeared in Desmog Canada (see desmog.ca/2013/05/08/unreported-emissions-natural-gas-blows-british-columbia-s-climate-action-plan-bc-s-carbon-footprint-likely-25-greater). The *Unburnable Carbon* report from the Grantham Institute is available at lse.ac.uk/GranthamInstitute/publication/unburnable-carbon-2013-wasted-capital-and-stranded-assets/. For peer-reviewed evidence that fossil fuel corporations have been key players in the climate change denial industry, see Dunlap and Jacques (2013). For analyses on the climate impacts of natural gas see Schrag (2012) and Howarth (2014).

My statement that we could be heading towards a world that is four and half degrees warmer than it was in pre-industrial times by 2100 is based on the RCP8.5 emissions scenario depicted in Figure SPM.10 of the *Summary for Policy Makers* of the 2013 IPCC report; see ipcc.ch/report/ar5/wg1/.

For insight into Port Metro Vancouver's disregard for public input into proposed coal port expansions, see realporthearings.org. Sources for figures regarding coal exports were:

- Cumulative capacity of existing and proposed coal ports in Vancouver, as of December 2013 (55 million metric tonnes): Voters Taking Action on Climate Change: vtacc.org/vtacc_template.php?content=export_campaign.
- Port Metro Vancouver coal exports (all types combined) in 2012 (32.7 million metric tonnes): Port Metro Vancouver's website in 2013 (the relevant webpage was no longer available in 2015).
- Carbon dioxide content of coal (2100.8 kilos of CO_2 per short ton of coal): US Energy Information Administration: eia.gov/environment/emissions/co2_vol_mass.cfm.
- British Columbia total greenhouse gas emissions in 2011 (61.5 million tonnes of CO_{2e}): British Columbia Ministry of

Environment: www2.gov.bc.ca/gov/content/environment/
climate-change/reports-data/provincial-ghg-inventory-
report-bc-s-pir.
- 65 percent of the world's coal plants must shut down by
2020: Rogelj et al. (2013).
- Global subsidies to energy industries in 2011 ($523
billion to fossil fuels vs. $88 billion to renewables): Interna-
tional Energy Agency's *World Energy Outlook Report* in 2012:
worldenergyoutlook.org/publications/weo-2012/#d
.en.26099.

For a review of Julian M. Allwood's work on how to reduce
consumption of metallurgical coal, see Allwood (2013). Mark Jacobson is quoted from his paper Jacobson and Delucchi (2011),
which is a good entry point into his renewable energy analyses.
Mark Jaccard is quoted from his article in the *Walrus*, thewalrus.
ca/the-accidental-activist/. My discussion of neoclassical and
ecological economics is based on Prugh et al. (1995), Costanza et
al. (1997) and the *Unburnable Carbon* 2013 report. Paul Hawken and
Robert Solow were quoted from Prugh et al. (1995). The statement
"2012 marked the 333rd consecutive month of above-average
global temperatures" is sourced from NOAA data, as reported in
Climate Central, climatecentral.org/news/november-was-333rd
-straight-month-with-above-average-temps-15361. Arms trade profits ($44 billion in 2011) are as shown in Figure 7 of the report by
the Federation of American Scientists, *Conventional Arms Transfers
to Developing Nations*, 2004–2011, available at fas.org/sgp/crs/
weapons/R42678.pdf. For more information on Kids For Climate
Action, see kidsforclimateaction.ca.

Mike Davis's article "Home-Front Ecology," describing the
powering down of the U.S. during World War II, was published
in the July/August 2007 issue of *Sierra*, vault.sierraclub.org/
sierra/200707/ecology.asp. Material and quotes from John Urry's
research are sourced from Urry (2013). For coverage of civil disobedience against the fossil fuels industry during November 2014

on Burnaby Mountain, see the many articles (including my own) in the *Vancouver Observer* (vancouverobserver.com/special-reports/tar-sands-reporting-project).

Material and quotes from Kevin Anderson regarding jet flying and carbon offsets are from Anderson (2012), my email correspondence with him and his blog, tyndall.ac.uk/online-tools/personal-blog/kevin-anderson-2. The last quote in the chapter is from Anderson and Bows (2012).

7. IRREVOCABLE CHANGE

This chapter derives primarily from personal experience, yet the following works provided additional subtext: Bill McKibben's book *Eaarth* (McKibben 2011); Andrew Zolli's essay "Good-Bye Sustainability, Hello Resilience," conservationmagazine.org/2013/03/good-bye-sustainability-hello-resilience/; and Roy Scranton's op-ed in the *New York Times* "Learning How to Die in the Anthropocene," opinionator.blogs.nytimes.com/2013/11/10/learning-how-to-die-in-the-anthropocene/?_r=1. The temperature time series graph I refer to is from a recent paper by Hansen and colleagues (Hansen et al. 2013). In typical Hansen fashion (and I say this admiringly), the paper's title—"Assessing 'Dangerous Climate Change': Required Reduction of Carbon Emissions to Protect Young People, Future Generations and Nature"—is more bold and direct than we usually see in academic journals. Thomas King is quoted from his book (and Massey Lectures) *The Truth About Stories*. For a short history of the Haida Gwaii blockades of 1985 and subsequent events, see the article in the *Haida Gwaii Observer*: qciobserver.com/Article.aspx?Id=6044.

Selected Bibliography

Alaback P.B. (1982). Dynamics of understory biomass in Sitka spruce-western hemlock forests of southeast Alaska. *Ecology*, 63, 1932–1948.

Alaback P.B. (1991). Comparative ecology of temperate rain-forests of the Americas along analogous climatic gradients. *Revista Chilena De Historia Natural*, 64, 399–412.

Allwood J.M. (2013). Transitions to material efficiency in the UK steel economy. *Philosophical Transactions of the Royal Society A: Mathematical, Physical and Engineering Sciences*, 371.

Anderson K. (2012). The inconvenient truth of carbon offsets. *Nature*, 484, 7.

Anderson K. & Bows A. (2012). A new paradigm for climate change. *Nature Climate Change*, 2, 639–640.

André C. & Platteau J.P. (1998). Land relations under unbearable stress: Rwanda caught in the Malthusian trap. *Journal of Economic Behavior & Organization*, 34, 1–47.

Anholt B.R. & Werner E.E. (1995). Interactions between food availability and predation mortality mediated by adaptive behavior. *Ecology*, 76, 2230–2234.

Berkeley S.A., Hixon M.A., Larson R.J. & Love M.S. (2004). Fisheries sustainability via protection of age structure and spatial distribution of fish populations. *Fisheries*, 29, 23–32.

Briceño C., Knapp L.A., Silva A., Paredes J., Avendano I., Vargas A., Sotomayor J. & Vila A.R. (2013). Detecting an increase in an endangered huemul *Hippocamelus bisulcus* population following removal of cattle and cessation of poaching in coastal Patagonia, Chile. *Oryx*, 47, 273–279.

Brody H. (2001). *The other side of Eden: Hunters, farmers and the shaping of the world.* Vancouver: Douglas & McIntyre.

Charpentier A.D., Bergerson J.A. & MacLean H.L. (2009). Understanding the Canadian oil sands industry's greenhouse gas emissions. *Environmental Research Letters*, 4, 1–11.

Cheung W.W.L., Sarmiento J.L., Dunne J., Frolicher T.L., Lam V.W.Y., Palomares M.L.D., Watson R. & Pauly D. (2013). Shrinking of fishes exacerbates impacts of global ocean changes on marine ecosystems. *Nature Climate Change*, 3, 254–258.

Connors B.M., Braun D.C., Peterman R.M., Cooper A.B., Reynolds J.D., Dill L.M., Ruggerone G.T. & Krkosek M. (2012). Migration links ocean-scale competition and local ocean conditions with exposure to farmed salmon to shape wild salmon dynamics. *Conservation Letters*, 5, 304–312.

Costanza R., dArge R., deGroot R., Farber S., Grasso M., Hannon B., Limburg K., Naeem S., Oneill R.V., Paruelo J., Raskin R.G., Sutton P. & vandenBelt M. (1997). The value of the world's ecosystem services and natural capital. *Nature*, 387, 253–260.

Coumou D. & Rahmstorf S. (2012). A decade of weather extremes. *Nature Climate Change*, 2, 491–496.

Cruikshank J. (2005). *Do glaciers listen? Local knowledge, colonial encounters, and social imagination*. Vancouver: UBC Press.

Dellinger D. (2011). *Love letter to the milky way* (2nd ed.). Ashland, OR: White Cloud Press.

Doney S.C., Ruckelshaus M., Duffy J.E., Barry J.P., Chan F., English C.A., Galindo H.M., Grebmeier J.M., Hollowed A.B., Knowlton N., Polovina J., Rabalais N.N., Sydeman W.J. & Talley L.D. (2012). Climate change impacts on marine ecosystems. In C.A. Carlson & S.J. Giovannoni (Eds.), *Annual Review of Marine Science, Vol 4* (pp. 11–37).

Drake D.C. & Naiman R.J. (2007). Reconstruction of pacific salmon abundance from riparian tree-ring growth. *Ecological Applications*, 17, 1523–1542.

Dunlap R.E. & Jacques P.J. (2013). Climate change denial books and conservative think tanks: Exploring the connection. *American Behavioral Scientist*, 57, 699–731.

Dyer G. (2008). *Climate wars: The fight for survival as the world overheats*. Toronto: Random House Canada.

Estes J.A., Tinker M.T. & Bodkin J.L. (2010). Using ecological function to develop recovery criteria for depleted species: Sea otters and kelp forests in the Aleutian Archipelago. *Conservation Biology*, 24, 852–860.

Ferrari M.C.O., Dixson D.L., Munday P.L., McCormick M.I., Meekan M.G., Sih A. & Chivers D.P. (2011). Intrageneric variation in antipredator responses of coral reef fishes affected by ocean acidification: Implications for climate change projections on marine communities. *Global Change Biology*, 17, 2980–2986.

Frid A. (1994). Observations on habitat use and social organization of a huemul *Hippocamelus bisulcus* coastal population in Chile. *Biological Conservation*, 67, 13–19.

Frid A. (1997). Vigilance by female Dall's sheep: Interactions between predation risk factors. *Animal Behaviour*, 53, 799–808.

Frid A. (1999). Huemul (*Hippocamelus bisulcus*) sociality at a periglacial site: Sexual aggregation and habitat effects on group size. *Canadian Journal of Zoology / Revue canadienne de zoologie*, 77, 1083–1091.

Frid A. (2001). Habitat use by endangered huemul (*Hippocamelus bisulcus*): Cattle, snow, and the problem of multiple causes. *Biological Conservation*, 100, 261–267.

Frid A., Burns J., Baker G.G. & Thorne R.E. (2009). Predicting synergistic effects of resources and predators on foraging decisions by juvenile Steller sea lions. *Oecologia*, 158, 775–786.

Frid A., Connors B., Cooper A.B. & Marliave J. (2013). Size-structured abundance relationships between upper- and mid-trophic level predators on temperate rocky reefs. *Ethology Ecology & Evolution*, 25, 253–268.

Frid A. & Heithaus M.R. (2010). Conservation and anti-predator behavior. In M.D. Breed & J. Moore (Eds.), *Encyclopedia of Animal Behavior* (pp. 366–376). Oxford: Academic Press.

Frid A. & Marliave J. (2010). Predatory fishes affect trophic cascades and apparent competition in temperate reefs. *Biology Letters*, 6, 533–536.

Frid A., Marliave J. & Heithaus M. (2012). Interspecific variation in life history relates to antipredator decisions by marine mesopredators on temperate reefs. *PLoS ONE* 7(6), e40083. doi:10.1371/journal.pone.0040083.

Golumbia T. (2000). Introduced species management in Haida Gwaii (Queen Charlotte Islands). In L. Darling (Ed.), *Proceedings of a conference on the biology and management of species and habitats at risk, Kamloops, B.C., 15–19 Feb., 1999, Volume One*. Victoria and Kamloops, BC: BC Ministry of Environment, Lands and Parks and University College of the Cariboo.

Hansen J. (2009). *Storms of my grandchildren*. New York: Bloomsbury.

Hansen J., Kharecha P., Sato M., Masson-Delmotte V., Ackerman F., et al. (2013). Assessing "dangerous climate change": Required reduction of carbon emissions to protect young people, future generations and nature. *PLoS ONE*, 8(12): e81648. doi:10.1371/ journal.pone.0081648.

Hansen J., Sato M. & Ruedy R. (2012). Perception of climate change. *Proceedings of the National Academy of Sciences of the United States of America*, 109, E2415-E2423.

Hauger J.S. (2012). Science, climate change, and the evolution of security policy in the Asia-Pacific Region. *Annual Meeting of the American Association for the Advancement of Science*.

Hazen E.L., Jorgensen S., Rykaczewski R.R., Bograd S.J., Foley D.G., Jonsen I.D., Shaffer S.A., Dunne J.P., Costa D.P., Crowder L.B. & Block B.A. (2013). Predicted habitat shifts of Pacific top predators in a changing climate. *Nature Climate Change*, 3, 234–238.

Heithaus M., Frid A., Wirsing A. & Worm B. (2008). Predicting ecological consequences of marine top predator declines. *Trends in Ecology and Evolution*, 23, 202–210.

Heithaus M.R., Frid A., Wirsing A.J., Dill L.M., Fourqurean J.W., Burkholder D., Thomson J. & Bejder L. (2007). State-dependent risk-taking by green sea turtles mediates top-down effects of tiger shark intimidation in a marine ecosystem. *Journal of Animal Ecology*, 76, 837–844.

Heithaus M.R., Wirsing A.J. & Dill L.M. (2012). The ecological importance of intact top-predator populations: A synthesis of 15 years of research in a seagrass ecosystem. *Marine and Freshwater Research*, 63, 1039–1050.

Higdon J.W., Hauser D.D.W. & Ferguson S.H. (2012). Killer whales (*Orcinus orca*) in the Canadian Arctic: Distribution, prey items, group sizes, and seasonality. *Marine Mammal Science*, 28, E93–E109.

Howarth R.W. (2014). A bridge to nowhere: Methane emissions and the greenhouse gas footprint of natural gas. *Energy Science & Engineering*, 2, 47–60.

Hsiang S.M., Meng K.C. & Cane M.A. (2011). Civil conflicts are associated with the global climate. *Nature*, 476, 438–441.

Hughes J. (1999). W. Eugene Smith. In *W. Eugene Smith: Aperture Masters of Photography*. Aperture Foundation.

Hutchings J.A. & Post J.R. (2013). Gutting Canada's Fisheries Act: No fishery, no fish habitat protection. *Fisheries*, 38, 497–501.

Jacobson M.Z. & Delucchi M.A. (2011). Providing all global energy with wind, water, and solar power, part I: Technologies, energy resources, quantities and areas of infrastructure, and materials. *Energy Policy*, 39, 1154–1169.

Jones N. (2011a). Heating up tensions. *Nature Climate Change*, 1, 327–329.

Jones N. (2011b). Rhythm and reason. *Nature*, 469, 33.

Kawaguchi S., Ishida A., King R., Raymond B., Waller N., Constable A., Nicol S., Wakita M. & Ishimatsu A. (2013). Risk maps for Antarctic krill under projected Southern Ocean acidification. *Nature Climate Change*, 3.

King T. (2003). *The truth about stories*. Toronto: House of Anansi.

Lima S.L. & Dill L.M. (1990). Behavioural decisions made under the risk of predation. *Canadian Journal of Zoology*, 68, 619–640.

Mangel M. & Clark C.W. (1988). *Dynamic modeling in behavioral ecology*. Princeton: Princeton University Press.

Marliave J.B., Conway K.W., Gibbs D.M., Lamb A. & Gibbs C. (2009). Biodiversity and rockfish recruitment in sponge gardens and bioherms of southern British Columbia, Canada. *Marine Biology*, 156, 2247–2254.

Martin J.L., Stockton S.A., Allombert S. & Gaston A.J. (2010). Top-down and bottom-up consequences of unchecked ungulate browsing on plant and animal diversity in temperate forests: Lessons from a deer introduction. *Biological Invasions*, 12, 353–371.

Matthews H.D. & Solomon S. (2013). Irreversible does not mean unavoidable. *Science*, 340, 438–439.

McKibben B. (2011). *Eaarth: Making life on a tough new planet* (2nd ed.). New York: St. Martin's Griffin.

Miller K.M., Teffer A., Tucker S., Li S.R., Schulze A.D., Trudel M., Juanes F., Tabata A., Kaukinen K.H., Ginther N.G., Ming T.J., Cooke S.J., Hipfner J.M., Patterson D.A. & Hinch S.G. (2014). Infectious disease, shifting climates, and opportunistic predators: Cumulative factors potentially impacting wild salmon declines. *Evolutionary Applications*, 7, 812–855.

Mirza M.M. (2012). Science for adaptation to climate change: The case of Bangladesh. *Annual Meeting of the American Association for the Advancement of Science*.

Montzka S.A., Dlugokencky E.J. & Butler J.H. (2011). Non-CO_2 greenhouse gases and climate change. *Nature*, 476, 43–50.

Moody M. & Pitcher T. (2010). Eulachon (*Thaleichthys pacificus*): past and present. Fisheries Centre Research Reports, 18, 197 pages.

Morato T., Watson R., Pitcher T.J. & Pauly D. (2006). Fishing down the deep. *Fish and Fisheries*, 7, 24–34.

Nikiforuk A. (2010). *Tar sands: Dirty oil and the future of a continent.* Vancouver: Greystone Books.

Oechel W.C., Hastings S.J., Vourlitis G., Jenkins M., Riechers G. & Grulke N. (1993). Recent change of Arctic tundra ecosystems from a net carbon-dioxide sink to a source. *Nature*, 361, 520–523.

Orbinski J. (2008). *An imperfect offering: Humanitarian action in the twenty-first century.* Toronto: Doubleday Canada.

Parenti C. (2011). *Tropic of chaos: Climate change and the new geography of violence.* New York: Nation Books.

Pauly D., Christensen V., Guénette S., Pitcher T.J., Sumaila U.R., Walters C.J., Watson R. & Zeller D. (2002). Towards sustainability in world fisheries. *Nature*, 418, 689–695.

Power S. (2002). *Problem from hell: America and the age of genocide.* New York: Harper Collins.

Prugh L.R., Stoner C.J., Epps C.W., Bean W.T., Ripple W.J., Laliberte A.S. & Brashares J.S. (2009). The rise of the mesopredator. *Bioscience*, 59, 779–791.

Prugh T., Constanza R., Cumberland J.H., Daly H., Goodland R. & Norgaard R. (1995). *Natural capital and human economic survival.* Sunderland, MA: Sinauer and Associates.

Quinn T.P., Carlson S.M., Gende S.M. & Rich H.B. (2009). Transportation of Pacific salmon carcasses from streams to riparian forests by bears. *Canadian Journal of Zoology / Revue canadienne de zoologie*, 87, 195–203.

Riihela A., Manninen T. & Laine V. (2013). Observed changes in the albedo of the Arctic sea-ice zone for the period 1982–2009. *Nature Climate Change*, 3, 895–898.

Rogelj J., McCollum D.L., O'Neill B.C. & Riahi K. (2013). 2020 emissions levels required to limit warming to below 2 degrees C. *Nature Climate Change*, 3, 405-412.

Rooney R.C., Bayley S.E. & Schindler D.W. (2012). Oil sands mining and reclamation cause massive loss of peatland and stored carbon. *Proceedings of the National Academy of Sciences of the United States of America*, 109, 4933–4937.

Rosa R. & Seibel B.A. (2008). Synergistic effects of climate-related variables suggest future physiological impairment in a top oceanic predator. *Proceedings of the National Academy of Sciences of the United States of America*, 105, 20776–20780.

Schmitz O. (2008). Effects of predator hunting mode on grassland ecosystem function. *Science*, 319, 952–954.

Schoen J.W. & Kirchhoff M.D. (1990). Seasonal habitat use by Sitka black-tailed deer on Admiralty Island, Alaska. *Journal of Wildlife Management*, 54, 371–378.

Schrag D.P. (2012). Is shale gas good for climate change? *Daedalus*, 141, 72–80.

Sinclair A.R.E. & Arcese P. (1995). Population consequences of predation-sensitive foraging: the Serengeti wildebeest. *Ecology*, 76, 882–891.

Six K.D., Kloster S., Ilyina T., Archer S.D., Zhang K. & Maier-Reimer E. (2013). Global warming amplified by reduced sulphur fluxes as a result of ocean acidification. *Nature Climate Change*, 3, 975–984.

Sloan N. & Dick L. (2012). *Sea Otters of Haida Gwaii: Icons in Human-Ocean Relations*. Queen Charlotte and Skidegate, BC: Archipelago Management Board and Haida Gwaii Museum.

Solomon S., Plattner G.K., Knutti R. & Friedlingstein P. (2009). Irreversible climate change due to carbon dioxide emissions. *Proceedings of the National Academy of Sciences of the United States of America*, 106, 1704–1709.

Stambuk P. (1986). *Rosa Yagán, el último eslabón*. Santiago: Editorial Andres Bello.

Stirling I. & Parkinson C. (2006). Possible effects of climate warming on selected populations of polar bears (*Ursus maritimus*) in the Canadian Arctic. *Arctic*, 59, 261–275.

Stouffer R.J. (2012). Oceanography: Future impact of today's choices. *Nature Climate Change*, 2, 397–398.

Swart N. & Weaver A. (2012). The Alberta oil sands and climate. *Nature Climate Change*, 2, 134–136.

Taylor S.G. (2008). Climate warming causes phenological shift in pink salmon, *Oncorhynchus gorbuscha*, behavior at Auke Creek, Alaska. *Global Change Biology*, 14, 229–235.

Toseland A., Daines S.J., Clark J.R., Kirkham A., Strauss J., Uhlig C., Lenton T.M., Valentin K., Pearson G.A., Moulton V. & Mock T. (2013). The impact of temperature on marine phytoplankton resource allocation and metabolism. *Nature Climate Change*, 3, 979–984.

Trebilco R. (2014). *Size-based insight into the structure and function of reef fish communities* (Unpublished doctoral dissertation). Simon Fraser University, Vancouver.

Trebilco R., Baum J., Salomon A. & Dulvy N. (2013). Ecosystem ecology: Size-based constraints on the pyramids of life. *Trends in Ecology & Evolution*, 28, 423–431.

Tripati A.K., Roberts C.D. & Eagle R.A. (2009). Coupling of CO_2 and ice sheet stability over major climate transitions of the last 20 million years. *Science*, 326, 1394–1397.

Turner C. (2013). *The war on science: Muzzled scientists and wilful blindness in Stephen Harper's Canada*. Vancouver: Greystone.

Turner N.J. (1998). *Plant technology of First Peoples in British Columbia*. Victoria: Royal BC Museum.

Tyedmers P.H., Watson R. & Pauly D. (2005). Fueling global fishing fleets. *Ambio*, 34, 635–638.

Urry J. (2013). A low carbon economy and society. *Philosophical Transactions of the Royal Society A: Mathematical, Physical and Engineering Sciences*, 371.

Vourc'h G., Martin J.L., Duncan P., Escarre J. & Clausen T.P. (2001). Defensive adaptations of *Thuja plicata* to ungulate browsing: A comparative study between mainland and island populations. *Oecologia*, 126, 84–93.

Watson J. & Estes J.A. (2011). Stability, resilience, and phase shifts in rocky subtidal communities along the west coast of Vancouver Island, Canada. *Ecological Monographs*, 81, 215–239.

Watson L. (1995). *Dark nature: A natural history of evil*. New York: Harper Collins.

Wilmers C., Estes J.A., Edwards M., Laidre K. & Konar B. (2012). Do trophic cascades affect the storage and flux of atmospheric carbon? An analysis of sea otters and kelp forests. *Frontiers in Ecology and the Environment*, 10, 409–415.

Wittmann A.C. & Portner H.-O. (2013). Sensitivities of extant animal taxa to ocean acidification. *Nature Climate Change*, 3, 995–1001.

Yannic G., Pellissier L., Ortego J., Lecomte N., Couturier S., Cuyler C., et al. (2014). Genetic diversity in caribou linked to past and future climate change. *Nature Climate Change*, 2013/12/15/online.

Zhang D., Brecke P., Lee H., He Y. & Zhang J. (2007). Global climate change, war, and population decline in recent human history. *Proceedings of the National Academy of Science*, 104, 19214–19219.

Photo Information

Cover: A celebratory meal of eulachon about to be consumed by Wuikinuxv people of British Columbia's central coast, May 2015. Eulachon, a species of smelt, are crucial to the cultural integrity of many coastal First Nations, yet have declined drastically since the early 1990s possibly because of the combined effects of climate change and trawl bycatch. In 2015, the Wuikinuxv Nation experienced their first strong eulachon run in twenty years—a major cause for celebration. Twyla Bella, Gail and I (in Wuikinuxv at the time for rockfish research) were lucky to partake in this meal.

Pages 4–5: Seven-year-old Twyla Bella at Hotspring Island, Haida Gwaii, July 2011. A break from our research on the ecology of rocky reefs.

Pages 8–9: Gail Lotenberg, my wife and Twyla Bella's mother, kayaking along the north end of Yakobi Island, southeast Alaska, May 1997.

Pages 12–13: Yearling female huemul, tidal glacier and iceberg-strewn fjord at my Fiordo Tempano study site, southern Chile, October 1990. Huemul are an endangered species of deer found only in the southern Andes.

Pages 22–23: Tidal glacier near the Beagle Channel, Tierra del Fuego, Chile, May 1990. This was a rare moment of calm weather during my solo kayak journey.

Pages 38–39: Dall's sheep mother and young, Sheep Mountain, Kluane National Park Reserve, Yukon, May 1993. This kind of scene encapsulates the great pleasure of studying the behavioural ecology of mountain ungulates.

Pages 54–55: Charlie Mason, whose traditional name is Neasmuutk Hai maas, heads out from Klemtu in his punt for a day of long-line fishing for halibut and rockfish, July 2014. Charlie is a hereditary chief of the Kitasoo/Xai'Xais Nation of British Columbia's central coast and a very influential mentor to me. He informs much of my ecological research in this part of the world.

Pages 74–75: Gail Lotenberg, my wife and Twyla Bella's mother, exhausted after a major crossing during our kayak trip through British Columbia's central coast, August 1994.

PAGES 90–91: Scallop fishermen take me for a ride in their small fishing boat, Tierra del Fuego, southern Chile, May 1989. Their company was a welcomed break during my solo kayak journey.

PAGES 94–95: A scene in the streets of Bella Bella, the community of British Columbia's central coast that is home to the Heiltsuk people, July 2014.

PAGE 96: Fording the frigid Watson River with eight-month-old Twyla Bella and about to enter the boreal forest to pick cranberries, collect meadow mushrooms and hunt grouse, southwest Yukon, October 2004. Gail Lotenberg photo

PAGE 97: Twyla Bella at eleven years old in Wuikinuxv, British Columbia's central coast, May 2015. As part of our research, she is measuring a canary rockfish. Natalie Ban photo

PAGES 98–99: This photo shows me ascending back to the upper kelp canopy at the end of a research dive on a pinnacle off the Tar Islands, southeastern Haida Gwaii, July 2009. A yellowtail rockfish is in the foreground. Rowan Trebilco photo

PAGE 100, TOP: Black rockfish in the upper canopy of a kelp forest in Haida Gwaii. This scene is typical of the many research dives I conducted on submerged pinnacles with my friend and colleague Rowan Trebilco. Rowan Trebilco photo

PAGE 100, BOTTOM: Black turnstones take flight from a rocky intertidal shore along British Columbia's central coast, August 1994.

PAGE 101: Here I am about to fillet a dinner catch of copper rockfish during the five-week kayak journey Gail and I made along British Columbia's central coast, August 1994. Gail Lotenberg photo

PAGE 102: Twyla Bella at age two and a half being helped by her friend, Ensio, onto a canoe on Annie Lake, southwestern Yukon, June 2006. A glimmer, to my biased eyes, of W. Eugene Smith's *A Walk To Paradise Garden*.

PAGE 103: Gail holds five-month-old Twyla Bella in the near-midnight sunset of southeast Alaska during summer solstice, Lynn Canal, Alaska, June 2004.

PAGES 104–105: Kitasoo/Xai'Xais people welcoming canoes visiting from First Nations communities in Haida Gwaii and the Skeena River region, Klemtu, British Columbia's central coast, July 2014.

PAGES 106–107: Twyla Bella at eight years old kayaking near Meares Island, Clayoqout Sound, southern coast of British Columbia, July 2012.

PAGE 108, TOP: Ernie Mason of the Kitasoo/Xai'Xais Nation handles a yelloweye rockfish during our research in Kitasu Bay, British Columbia's central coast, August 2013. His wife Sandie Hankewich and their daughter Jesse (one year old at the time) are in the background.

PAGE 108, BOTTOM: Xeni Gwet'in people butcher a mule deer, vicinity of Chilko River, southwestern British Columbia, August 2014.

PAGE 109, TOP: Gilbert Salomon of the Xeni Gwet'in Nation and his grand-daughter eating saskatoon berries near their home by Chilko Lake, Nemiah Valley, southwestern British Columbia, August 2012.

PAGE 109, BOTTOM: Six-year-old Twyla Bella during our canoe journey down the Fraser River, southwestern British Columbia, October 2010. She is sitting by Bobbi Peters from the Chawathil Nation.

PAGES 110–111: Gail Lotenberg at Lynn Canal, southeast Alaska during late spring, mid-1990s.

PAGES 112–113: Julianna Lulua of the Xeni Gwet'in Nation stands in a smoke-house amidst freshly caught sockeye salmon and just-butchered mule deer. Vicinity of Chilko River, southwestern British Columbia, August 2014.

PAGES 114–115: Gilbert Salomon of the Xeni Gwet'in Nation near his home by Chilko Lake, August 2012.

PAGE 116: Willow ptarmigan in winter, southwest Yukon, mid-1990s.

PAGE 117: Firth River, northern Yukon, July 1997.

PAGE 118: Richardson Mountains, Northwest Territories, August 1987.

PAGE 119, TOP: Hoge Pass, Kluane National Park Reserve, July 1998. This was the study site for some of my research on Dall's sheep.

PAGE 119, BOTTOM: Gail and eighteen-month-old Twyla Bella on ridges above the Watson River and Wheaton River watersheds near our home at the time, southwest Yukon, September 2005.

PAGES 120–121: Dall's sheep on Sheep Mountain, Kluane National Park Reserve, Yukon, during the research I conducted in the late winter of 1993.

PAGES 122, TOP: Richardson Mountains, Northwest Territories, August 1987.

PAGES 122, BOTTOM: A scene from ridges above the Ecstall River watershed, northwest British Columbia, August 1993. The vast amounts of late summer snow and ice in this image is something that I took for granted back then.

These days I wonder how much snow and ice I would see if I was to return to the same viewpoint at the same time of year, twenty-two years further into climate change.

PAGE 123: Unable to use the engine in these conditions, Puerto Edén residents Victor Oswaldo Muñoz and Victor Manuel Zuñiga row the vessel Lorena through the icebergs of Fiordo Tempano while shuttling our research crew between huemul study sites, southern Chile, October 1995.

PAGE 124: Huemul buck in Fiordo Tempano, southern Chile, 1990. This was one of twenty-two individuals we could recognize by antler shape and coat markings during the course of our research that year.

PAGE 125: Guachipato, who was instrumental to my huemul research, by his home in Puerto Edén, southern Chile, 1990.

PAGES 126–127: Fiordo Tempano, southern Chile, 1990. This was the everyday view we lived with during huemul research.

PAGES 128: A chum salmon, dead after spawning, on the Kynoch River, August 2013.

PHOTO: GAIL LOTENBERG

ABOUT THE AUTHOR

Dr. Alejandro Frid is an ecologist for First Nations of British Columbia's Central Coast, and an adjunct assistant professor in Environmental Studies at the University of Victoria. Working at the interface of conservation science and social justice for over two decades, his research experience has spanned from conflicts between industrial development and terrestrial wildlife to the plight of endangered species and the effects of overfishing on marine predators. Born and raised in Mexico City, twice arrested for civil disobedience against fossil fuel companies and their climate-destroying emissions, and spending his adult life in British Columbia and the Yukon, he inhabits the worlds of science, modern indigenous cultures and climate activism.